# Study Guide

**Arlene Lundquist**
Utica College

**Lisa Bauer**
Utica College

**Kimberly J. Robinson**
Saint Mary's University

# The World of Psychology

## Fifth Canadian Edition

**Samuel E. Wood**
**Ellen Green Wood**
**Eileen Wood**
**Serge Desmarais**

PEARSON

**Toronto**

ISBN–13: 978-0-205-53524-8
ISBN–10:     0-205-53524-8

Executive Acquisitions Editor: Ky Pruesse
Senior Developmental Editor: Jennifer Murray
Production Editor: Amanda Wesson
Production Coordinator: Janis Raisen
Composition: Christine Velakis


3 4 5     11 10  09


Printed and bound in Canada.

# TABLE OF CONTENTS

# PREFACE

## HOW TO USE
## THIS STUDY GUIDE

Invest your time so you get the greatest benefit!

The following techniques have been shown to increase a student's mastery of new information:

- Use as many of your senses and abilities as possible—writing, reading, hearing, speaking, drawing, etc.

- Organize information so it is meaningful to you.

- Study with other people whenever possible.

- Have FUN. We remember what we enjoy.

# CHAPTER OUTLINE

## Class and Text Notes

This section is designed so you can take notes on these pages during lectures and also from your reading of the text. Most students find it useful to read the text and make notes before the instructor covers the material in class.

Before you begin filling out this section decide how you will tell the difference between
- your ideas
- lecture notes
- concepts from the text
- topics emphasized on the exam

The use of different colours of pens can help you differentiate each area.

## Chapter Learning Objectives

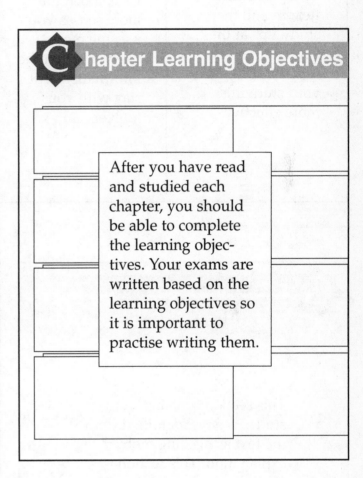

After you have read and studied each chapter, you should be able to complete the learning objectives. Your exams are written based on the learning objectives so it is important to practise writing them.

## Practice Multiple-Choice Test

Practice exams are an important way to check your progress. After studying the text and completing the Study Guide activities, answer these questions to determine if you need to review any areas before your exam. Answer the multiple-choice questions early enough so if you are confused about any concepts, you still have time to ask for clarification from the instructor, a tutor, or your classmates.

## Study Tips

There are study tips in the first nine chapters. These tips can help you take better notes and do better on exams. Reading all the study tips at the beginning of the semester can make your studying more effective.

## Try It

The TRY IT columns apply several of your senses to the topic in the chapter. Remember, the more senses you use, the more likely it is that the information will stay with you forever.

During times of stress, flash cards can serve a very useful function. Stress is much worse when we feel overwhelmed; in fact, we tend to shut down and do nothing. At those times divide up your tasks and do a small portion every day. Studying 10 flash cards today is less overwhelming than thinking about 100 pages covered on your next exam.

## Glossary for Text Language Enhancement

This section contains words students have identified from the text as needing more explanation. This section is for anyone who can benefit from extra support in English.

This page can be cut out, folded in half, and used as a bookmark in the appropriate chapter.

## Cut-Out Vocabulary Cards

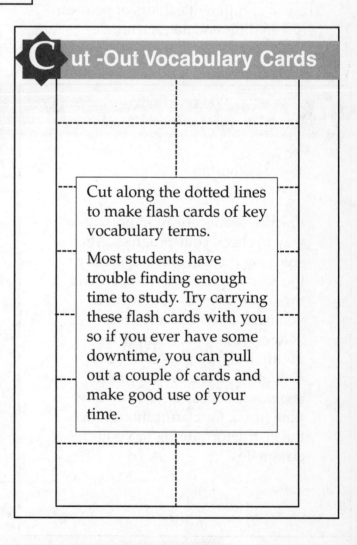

Cut along the dotted lines to make flash cards of key vocabulary terms.

Most students have trouble finding enough time to study. Try carrying these flash cards with you so if you ever have some downtime, you can pull out a couple of cards and make good use of your time.

# INTRODUCTION TO PSYCHOLOGY

## CHAPTER OUTLINE

This outline provides a way to organize your notes from both the text and the lecture. It will also serve as a review for the exam.

| Module 1.1 Introduction to Psychology | 1. Psychology: Science or Common Sense? |
| | 2. The Goals of Psychology |
| | 3. What Is a Theory? |
| | 4. Basic and Applied Research |

| Module 1.2<br>Descriptive<br>Research<br>Methods | 1. Naturalistic Observation: Caught in the Act of Being Themselves |
|---|---|
| | 2. Laboratory Observation: A More Scientific Look at the Participant |
| | 3. The Case Study Method: Studying a Few Participants in Depth |
| | 4. Survey Research: The Art of Sampling and Questioning |
| Module 1.3<br>The<br>Experimental<br>Method:<br>Searching for<br>Causes | 1. Independent and Dependent Variables |
| | 2. Experimental and Control Groups: The Same Except for the Treatment |
| | 3. Control in the Experiment: Attempting to Rule Out Chance |
| | 4. Generalizing the Experimental Findings:<br>Do the Findings Apply to Other Groups? |
| | 5. Potential Problems in Experimental Research |
| | 6. Advantages and Limitations of the Experimental Method |

| Module 1.4 Other Research Methods | 1. The Correlational Method: Discovering Relationships, Not Causes 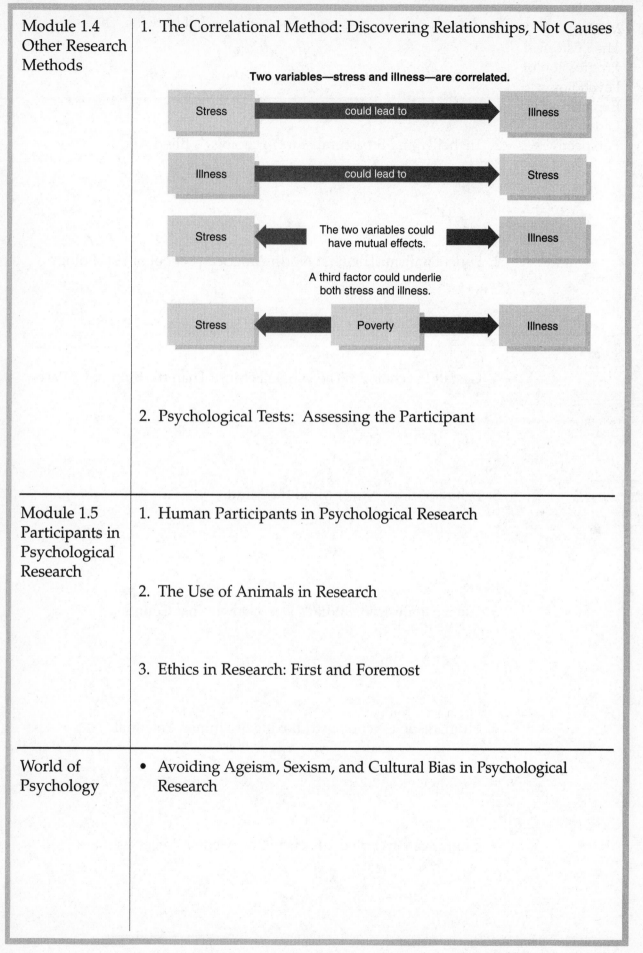 2. Psychological Tests: Assessing the Participant |
|---|---|
| Module 1.5 Participants in Psychological Research | 1. Human Participants in Psychological Research 2. The Use of Animals in Research 3. Ethics in Research: First and Foremost |
| World of Psychology | • Avoiding Ageism, Sexism, and Cultural Bias in Psychological Research |

Module 1.6
The Historical
Progression of
Psychology:
Exploring the
Different
Perspectives

1. Wilhelm Wundt: The Founding of Psychology

2. Titchener and Structuralism: Psychology's Blind Alley

3. Functionalism: The First North American School of Psychology

4. Gestalt Psychology: The Whole Is More Than the Sum of Its Parts

5. Behaviourism: Never Mind the Mind

6. Psychoanalysis: It's What's Deep Down That Counts

7. Humanistic Psychology: Looking at Human Potential

8. Cognitive Psychology: Focusing on Mental Processes

| Module 1.7 Psychology Today | 1. Current Perspectives in Psychology: Views on Behaviour and Thinking |
|---|---|

1. Current Perspectives in Psychology: Views on Behaviour and Thinking

   a. *Biological Perspective*: It's What's Inside That Counts

   b. *Evolutionary Perspective:* Adapting to the Environment

   c. *Sociocultural Perspective:* The Cultural Impact of Our World

2. Psychologists at Work

   What are some specialties in psychology, and in what settings are they employed?

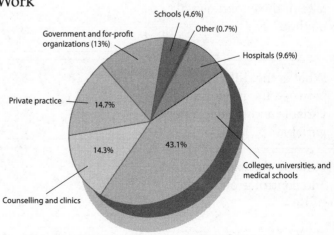

# Chapter Learning Objective Questions

Answer the following questions in the space provided and check your answers on the page numbers listed.

| | |
|---|---|
| 1.1 What are the four goals of psychology? p. 5 | |
| 1.2 What is the difference between basic and applied research? p. 6 | |
| 1.3 What is naturalistic observation, and what are some of its advantages and limitations? p. 7 | |
| 1.4 What is the case study method, and for what purposes is it particularly well suited? p. 8 | |
| 1.5 What are the methods and purposes of survey research? p. 8 | |
| 1.6 What is a representative sample, and why is it essential in a survey? p. 8 | |
| 1.7 What is the main advantage of the experimental method? p. 9 | |
| 1.8 What is the difference between the independent variable and the dependent variable? p. 10 | |
| 1.9 How do the experimental and control groups differ? p. 10 | |
| 1.10 What is selection bias, and what technique do researchers use to control for it? p. 11 | |

1.11 What is the placebo effect, and how do researchers control for it? p. 12

1.12 What is experimenter bias, and how is it controlled? p. 12

1.13 What is the correlational method, and when is it used? p. 13

1.14 What is a correlation coefficient? p. 14

1.15 Why are animals used in research? p. 16

1.16 What are some ethical guidelines governing the use of human participants in research? p. 18

1.17 What was Wilhelm Wundt's contribution to psychology? p. 19

1.18 What were the goals and method of structuralism, the first school of psychology? p. 19–20

1.19 What was the goal of the early school of psychology known as functionalism? p. 20

1.20 What is the emphasis of Gestalt psychology? p. 22

| 1.21 How did behaviourism differ from previous schools of psychology? p. 21 | |
| --- | --- |
| 1.22 What was the role of the unconscious in psycho-analysis, Freud's approach to psychology? p. 21 | |
| 1.23 What is the focus of humanistic psychology? p. 22 | |
| 1.24 What is the focus of cognitive psychology? p. 22 | |
| 1.25 What is the focus of the biological perspective? p. 24 | |
| 1.26 What is the focus of the evolutionary perspective? p. 24 | |
| 1.27 What is the focus of the sociocultural perspective? p. 24 | |
| 1.28 What are some specialties in psychology, and in what settings are they employed? p. 24 | |
| | |
| | |

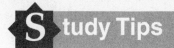 

Learn to study more effectively and improve your memory with these tips and practical exercises.

## Improving Your Memory

1. Learn general first and then specific.

2. Make material meaningful to you.

3. Create associations with what you already know.

4. Learn it actively.

5. Imagine vivid pictures.

6. Recite aloud.

7. Reduce noise and interruptions.

8. Overlearn the material.

9. Be aware of your attitude toward information.

10. Space out learning over several days.

11. Remember related information when you are having trouble recalling something.

12. Use mnemonic devices (rhymes or words created from material).

13. Combine several of these techniques at once.

## Naturalistic Observations on Campus

Try answering the following questions to experience being a researcher in naturalistic observation.

1. Go to the study areas of the library. Do you see more men or women studying there? (This may help you decide where you want to study.)

2. What is the average distance between two men walking together across campus? Does this differ for women or various ethnic groups?

3. What is the average group size of students in the cafeteria?

4. How could the information from question #3 be used by the management of the cafeteria?

5. Observe students talking. What conclusions can you make about differences among students with regard to eye contact, distance between them, and body language?

## Use the SQ3R Method when studying your text

### Survey

Before you read the chapter, take a visual tour of it. Notice the headings and how the material is organized. Observe tables and figures and other boxed material in the text. Read the introduction and summary statements.

### Question

While you are surveying the chapter, create questions along the way. Ask yourself what questions the material appears to be addressing. If you like, write down the questions. Now you are ready to begin reading your text.

### Read

Keep in mind the questions you have formulated and, as you read, seek answers to those questions. Notice bolded and italicized text, and reread complex material several times if necessary for comprehension. Divide your reading task into sections.

### Recite

At the end of each reading section, recite the material. Take notes in your own words or even say it out loud. You can recite to a friend, a tape recorder, or yourself. This will help you encode the information more efficiently so it is easier to retrieve at test time.

### Review

At the end of the chapter, you should go back and review all that you have learned. Develop mnemonics for anything that needs to be memorized. Use flash cards for anything that requires further practice and repetition. Go over material you found particularly difficult.

After studying the text and completing the Study Guide activities, answer these questions to determine if you need to review any areas before your exam.

1. Basic research is to _____ as applied research is to _____.
   a. simple; hard
   b. general knowledge; practical solutions
   c. important; frivolous
   d. scientific; intuitive

2. Naturalistic observation, the case study method, and the survey method share which of the following features?
   a. They all are descriptive research methods.
   b. None are used in physics.
   c. They each apply to limited situations.
   d. They all utilize correlation methods.

3. _____ occurs when researchers' expectations about a situation cause them to see what they expect to see or to make incorrect inferences about the behaviour they observe.
   a. Inferential bias
   b. Experimenter bias
   c. Selection bias
   d. Situational bias

4. Psychologists use _____ to gather in-depth information about a single individual.
   a. the case study method
   b. the survey method
   c. laboratory observation
   d. naturalistic observation

5. A group of participants selected for a survey from a population are referred to as a:
   a. subpopulation.
   b. sample.
   c. subgroup.
   d. control group.

6. The total group of people to which the researchers intend to generalize their results is called the:
   a. subpopulation.
   b. control group.
   c. population.
   d. subgroup.

7. Which is an advantage of using the survey method?
   a. Large numbers of subjects can be used.
   b. Answers are usually honest and accurate.
   c. A representative sample is fairly easy to obtain.
   d. A cause-and-effect relationship can be demonstrated.

8. Which of the following research methods yields the most definite evidence of cause and effect?
   a. naturalistic observation
   b. the survey method
   c. the case study method
   d. the experimental method

9. What factor is manipulated by the researcher to determine its effect on a condition or behaviour?
   a. dependent variable
   b. independent variable
   c. control variable
   d. random variable

10. Dependent variable is to _____ as independent variable is to _____.
    a. cause; effect
    b. correlation; experiment
    c. effect; cause
    d. random; control

11. Participants are assigned to take math tests in either a warm classroom or a cold classroom. Test scores are then examined to determine whether these conditions affected performance. In this example, the independent variable is:
    a. mathematics skill.
    b. test scores.
    c. classroom temperature.
    d. not identified.

12. The _____ group of participants is exposed to the independent variable.
    a. sample
    b. population
    c. experimental group
    d. control group

13. Which of the following statements is NOT true about a control group?
    a. It should be similar to an experimental group.
    b. It is exposed to the independent variable.
    c. At the end of the experiment, it is measured on the dependent variable.
    d. It is used for purposes of comparison.

14. Participant _____ is involved with the placebo effect.
    a. hypothesis
    b. idea of how other participants behave
    c. experience of actual treatment
    d. expectation

15. When the new drug was tested, neither the researcher nor the patients knew who was getting the new drug and who was getting a sugar pill that looked like the drug. This control was know as:
    a. random assignment.
    b. the self-fulfilling prophecy.
    c. the single-blind technique.
    d. the double-blind technique.

16. Predicting that changes in one factor are associated with changes in another can best be determined using:
    a. naturalistic observation.
    b. laboratory observation.
    c. the case study method.
    d. the correlational method.

17. Reliability refers to:
    a. the ability of a test to measure what it is supposed to measure.
    b. the consistency of a test.
    c. how often researchers can expect a test to be right.
    d. the degree of relationship of the test to another, separate factor.

18. Validity refers to:
    a. the ability of a test to measure what it is supposed to measure.
    b. how often researchers can expect a test to be right.
    c. the consistency of a test.
    d. the degree of relationship of the test to another, separate factor.

19. Which of the following correlation coefficients indicates the strongest relationship?
    a. .00
    b. +.40
    c. +.75
    d. −.76

20. Who is used most often in experiments?
    a. young children in daycare settings
    b. college students
    c. paid adult volunteers
    d. members of the lower socioeconomic class

21. Ageism occurs when clinicians:
    a. treat all age groups with the same level of openness and respect.
    b. make assumptions about the differences between men and women.
    c. select younger clients over middle-aged clients.
    d. are open to working with clients of any age group.

22. Which of the following would a behaviourist NOT consider a subject for psychological study?
    a. interpersonal interactions
    b. problem-solving
    c. thinking
    d. public speaking

23. The major emphasis of psychoanalysis is:
    a. the uniqueness of human beings and their capacity for conscious choice and growth.
    b. the perception of whole units or patterns.
    c. the scientific study of behaviour.
    d. the unconscious.

# nswers to Multiple-Choice Questions

| Question Number | Answer | Learning Objective | Explanation for application questions |
|---|---|---|---|
| 1. | b. | 1.2 | Basic research seeks to acquire knowledge whereas applied research seeks resolution to particular problems. |
| 2. | a. | 1.2 | Descriptive research methods summarize data gathered in non-experimental ways. |
| 3. | b. | 1.12 | |
| 4. | a. | 1.4 | Case histories involve the in-depth study of a person or small group of people over an extended time. |
| 5. | b. | 1.6 | |
| 6. | c. | 1.6 | |
| 7. | a. | 1.5 | A list of questions can be given to a large number of people. |
| 8. | d. | 1.7 | Only experimental methods can show cause and effect. |
| 9. | b. | 1.8 | The dependent variable is the effect of the independent variable. |
| 10. | c. | 1.8 | |
| 11. | c. | 1.8 | The researcher manipulates the classroom temperature, so this is the independent variable. |
| 12. | c. | 1.9 | The experimental group receives the treatment of the independent variable. |
| 13. | b. | 1.9 | The control group does not receive the treatment. |
| 14. | d. | 1.11 | |
| 15. | d. | 1.12 | In a double-blind study neither the participant nor the researcher knows who has received the treatment. |
| 16. | d. | 1.14 | Correlational method allows one to predict changes in two associated factors. |
| 17. | b. | 1.14 | |
| 18. | a. | 1.14 | |
| 19. | d. | 1.14 | The closer to 1.0 (+ or –) the correlation coefficient is, the stronger the relationship. |
| 20. | b. | 1.15 | College students are often used in research because they are so convenient to use. |
| 21. | c. | 1.16 | |
| 22. | c. | 1.21 | Behaviourists believe that research should involve observable behaviours only. |
| 23. | d. | 1.22 | |

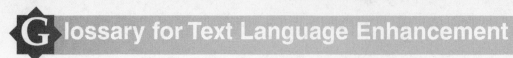

Students identified the following words from the text as needing more explanation. This page can be cut out, folded in half, and used as a bookmark for this chapter.

| term | definition |
| --- | --- |
| phenomenon | a factor or event that can be studied |
| alliances | a close association among people or nations |
| fascination | strong attraction |
| imperfections | flaws or errors in something |
| conception | the beginning of something |
| thrill-seekers | people who look for exciting activities |
| framework | the set of main ideas in a theory |
| real-world | actual; practical |
| inferences | making a conclusion |
| soliciting | asking for something, e.g. help |
| confederate | someone who works for the researcher |
| sophisticated | very developed, or complex |
| manipulates | controls |
| a self-fulfilling prophecy | expected outcome occurs |
| arbitrarily | based on one's personal choice, may be without supporting evidence |
| vocational interests | occupational interests |
| aptitude | ability |
| in conjunction with | connected with |
| ubiquitous | seeming to be present everywhere at the same time |
| deterioration | break down |
| minimize | reduce |
| deficit | lower than expected level of performance |
| deception | the act of misleading |
| debriefed | told about the experiment |
| misconceptions | misunderstandings |
| profoundly | very importantly |
| introspection | to look inside |
| proponents | people supporting a certain point of view |
| traumatic | resulting from an emotional experience or shock |
| hierarchy | the structure of |
| interdisciplinary | bringing together different ways of studying a problem, e.g., psychology, sociology, and medicine |
| parallel processing | two or more things being worked on at the same time |

| term | definition |
|------|------------|
| spurred | encouraged |
| dispositions | a person's nature or way of being |

# Thinking Critically

## Evaluation

Consider the three major forces in psychology: behaviourism, psychoanalysis, and humanistic psychology. Which do you like most? Which do you like least? Explain.

## Point/Counterpoint

This chapter discussed the issue of deception in research. Prepare convincing arguments to support each of these opinions:

a. Deception is justified in research studies.

b. Deception is not justified in research studies.

## Psychology in Your Life

In this chapter you've learned something about experimental research and survey research. How will this new knowledge affect the way you evaluate research studies in articles you read or in reports you hear in the future?

| | |
|---|---|
| psychology | survey |
| theory | population |
| basic research | sample |
| applied research | representative sample |
| descriptive research methods | experimental method |
| naturalistic observation | hypothesis |
| case study | independent variable |

| | |
|---|---|
| A method in which researchers use interviews and/or questionnaires to gather information about the attitudes, beliefs, experiences, or behaviours of a group of people. | The scientific study of behaviour and mental processes. |
| The entire group of interest to researchers and to which they wish to generalize their findings; the group from which a sample is selected. | A general principle or set of principles proposed in order to explain how a number of separate facts are related to one another. |
| The portion of any population that is selected for study and from which generalizations are made about the larger population. | Research conducted for the purpose of advancing knowledge rather than for its practical application. |
| A sample of participants selected from the larger population so important subgroups are included in the sample in the same proportions as found in the population. | Research conducted for the purpose of solving practical problems. |
| Research method in which researchers randomly assign participants to groups and control all conditions other than one or more independent variables, which are then manipulated to determine their effect. | Research methods that yield descriptions of behaviour rather than causal explanations. |
| A prediction about the relationship between two or more variables. | A research method in which the researcher observes and records behaviour in its natural setting, without attempting to influence or control it. |
| In an experiment the factor or condition that the researcher manipulates in order to determine its effect on another behaviour or condition known as the independent variable. | An in-depth study of one or a few participants consisting of information gathered through observation, interview, and perhaps psychological testing. |

| | |
|---|---|
| experimental group | double-blind technique |
| control group | correlational method |
| selection bias | correlation coefficient |
| random assignment | reliability |
| placebo effect | validity |
| placebo | dependent variable |
| experimenter bias | |

| | |
|---|---|
| An experimental procedure in which neither the participants nor the experimenter know who is in the experimental or control groups until after the results have been gathered. | In an experiment, a group that is exposed to the independent variable or treatment. |
| A research method used to establish the relationship between two characteristics, events, or behaviours. | In an experiment, a group that is similar to the experimental group and is exposed to the same experimental environment but is not exposed to the independent variable; used for purposes of comparison. |
| A numerical value that indicates the strength and direction of the relationship between two variables; ranges from +1.00 (a perfect positive correlation) to –1.00 (a perfect negative correlation). | The assignment of participants to experimental or control groups in such a way that systematic differences among the groups are present at the beginning of the experiment. |
| The ability of a test to yield nearly the same scores when the same people are tested and then retested using the same test or an alternative form of the test. | In an experiment, the assignment of participants to experimental and control groups by using a chance procedure. |
| The ability of a test to measure what it is intended to measure. | The phenomenon that occurs when a person's response to a treatment or response on the dependent variable in an experiment is due to expectations regarding the treatment rather than to the treatment itself. |
| The variable that is measured at the end of an experiment. It is presumed to vary as a result of the independent variable. | An inert substance, such as a sugar pill or an injection of saline solution, given to the control group in an experiment as a control for the placebo effect. |
| | A phenomenon that occurs when the researcher's preconceived notions in some way influence the participants' behaviour and/or the interpretation of experimental results. |

| | |
|---|---|
| structuralism | biological perspective |
| functionalism | |
| behaviourism | |
| psychoanalysis | |
| Gestalt psychology | |
| humanistic psychology | evolutionary perspective |
| cognitive psychology | sociocultural perspective |

| | |
|---|---|
| A perspective that emphasizes the role of biological processes and heredity as the key to understanding behaviour. | The first formal school of psychology, aimed at analyzing the basic elements, or structure of conscious mental experience though the use of introspection. |
| | An early school of psychology that was concerned with how mental processes help humans and animals adapt to their environments; developed in the United States as a reaction against structuralism. |
| | The school of psychology founded by John B. Watson that views observable, measurable behaviour as the appropriate subject matter for psychology and emphasizes the key role of environment as a determinant of behaviour. |
| | The term Freud used for both his theory of personality and his therapy for the treatment of psychological disorders; the unconscious is the primary focus. |
| | The school of psychology that emphasizes that individuals perceive objects and patterns as whole units and that the perceived whole is greater than the sum of its parts. |
| A perspective that focuses on how humans have evolved and adapted behaviours required for survival against various environmental pressures over the long course of evolution. | The school of psychology that focuses on the uniqueness of human beings and their capacity for choice, growth, and psychological health. |
| A perspective that emphasizes social and cultural influences on human behaviour and stresses the importance of understanding those influences when we interpret the behaviour of others. | A speciality that studies mental processes such as memory, problem solving, decision making, perception, language, and other forms of cognition; often uses the information-processing approach. |

# BIOLOGY AND BEHAVIOUR

This outline provides a way to organize your notes from both the text and the lecture. It will also serve as a review for the exam.

**Module 2.1
The Neurons
and the Neuro-
transmitters**

1.  The Neurons: Billions of Brain Cells

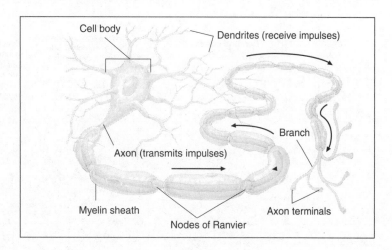

**The Action Potential**

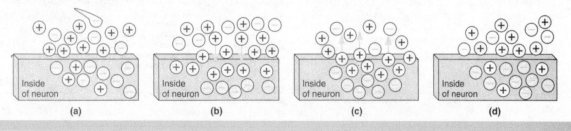

2. Neurotransmitters: The Chemical Messengers of the Brain

3. The Variety of Neurotransmitters: Some Excite and Some Inhibit

Module 2.2
The Central
Nervous
System

1. The Spinal Cord: An Extension of the Brain

2. The Brainstem: The Most Primitive Part of the Brain

3. The Cerebellum: A Must for Graceful Movement

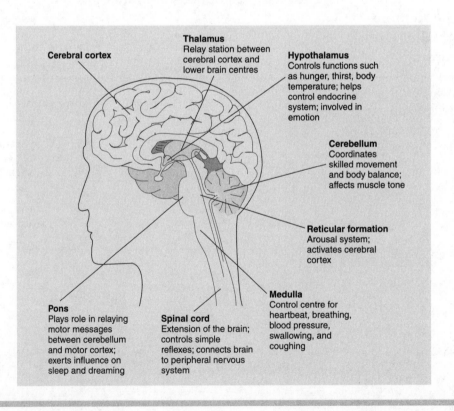

**Cerebral cortex**

**Thalamus**
Relay station between
cerebral cortex and
lower brain centres

**Hypothalamus**
Controls functions such
as hunger, thirst, body
temperature; helps
control endocrine
system; involved in
emotion

**Cerebellum**
Coordinates
skilled movement
and body balance;
affects muscle tone

**Reticular formation**
Arousal system;
activates cerebral
cortex

**Medulla**
Control centre for
heartbeat, breathing,
blood pressure,
swallowing, and
coughing

**Pons**
Plays role in relaying
motor messages
between cerebellum
and motor cortex;
exerts influence on
sleep and dreaming

**Spinal cord**
Extension of the brain;
controls simple
reflexes; connects brain
to peripheral nervous
system

4. The Thalamus: The Relay Station between Lower and Higher Brain Centres

5. The Hypothalamus: A Master Regulator

6. The Limbic System: Primitive Emotion and Memory

**Module 2.3 The Cerebral Hemispheres**

1. The Lobes of the Brain

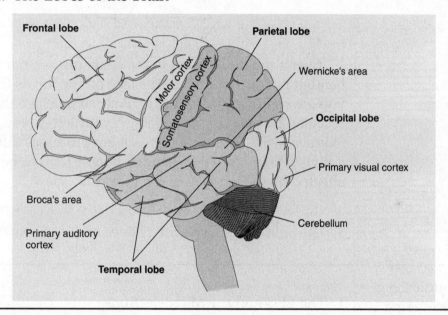

Frontal lobe

Parietal lobe

Motor cortex

Somatosensory cortex

Wernicke's area

**Occipital lobe**

Primary visual cortex

Broca's area

Cerebellum

Primary auditory cortex

**Temporal lobe**

**Module 2.4 Specialization of the Cerebral Hemispheres**

1. Functions of the Left Hemisphere: Language First and Foremost

2. Functions of the Right Hemisphere: The Leader in Visual-Spatial Tasks

### Try It!
### Testing the Hemispheres

Get a metre stick or yardstick. Try balancing it across your left hand and then across your right hand. Most people are better with their dominant hand. Is this true for you?

Now try this: Begin reciting the alphabet out loud as fast as you can while balancing the stick with your left hand. Do you have less trouble this time? Why? The right hemisphere controls the act of balancing with the left hand. However, your left hemisphere, though poor at controlling the left hand, still tries to coordinate your balancing efforts. When you distract the left hemisphere with a steady stream of talk, the right hemisphere can orchestrate more efficient balancing with your left hand, without interference.

## Handedness and Perception

Pick out the happy face and the sad face.

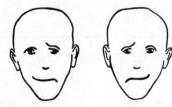

Even though the faces in the drawings are mirror images, right-handed people tend to see the face on the left as the happier face. If you are right-handed, you are likely to perceive the emotional tone revealed by the part of the face to your left as you view it (McGee & Skinner, 1987). The right hemisphere processes information from the left visual field, so right-handed people tend to be more emotionally affected by the left side of the faces they view.

3. The Split Brain: Separate Halves or Two Separate Brains?

| | |
|---|---|
| Module 2.5 Discovering the Brain's Mysteries | 1. The EEG and the Microelectrode |
| | 2. The CT Scan and MRI |
| | 3. The PET Scan, the Functional MRI, and Other Imaging Techniques |
| Module 2.6 The Brain across the Lifespan | 1. Brain Damage: Causes and Consequences |

| Module 2.7 The Peripheral Nervous System | 1. The Somatic Nervous System |
|---|---|

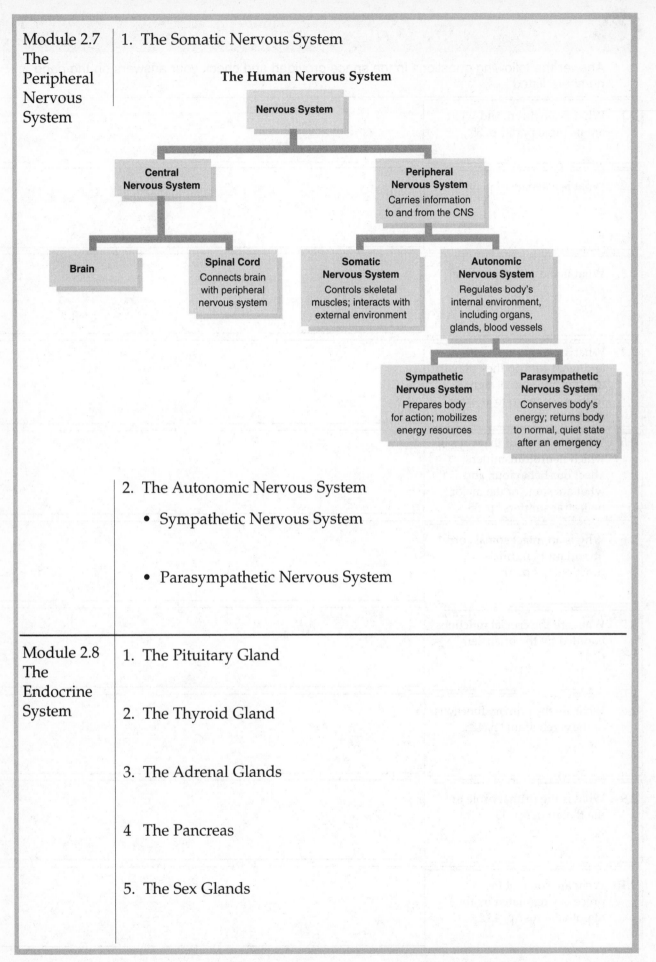

**The Human Nervous System**

Nervous System

Central Nervous System

Peripheral Nervous System
Carries information to and from the CNS

Brain

Spinal Cord
Connects brain with peripheral nervous system

Somatic Nervous System
Controls skeletal muscles; interacts with external environment

Autonomic Nervous System
Regulates body's internal environment, including organs, glands, blood vessels

Sympathetic Nervous System
Prepares body for action; mobilizes energy resources

Parasympathetic Nervous System
Conserves body's energy; returns body to normal, quiet state after an emergency

2. The Autonomic Nervous System

- Sympathetic Nervous System

- Parasympathetic Nervous System

| Module 2.8 The Endocrine System | 1. The Pituitary Gland |
|---|---|

2. The Thyroid Gland

3. The Adrenal Glands

4  The Pancreas

5. The Sex Glands

# Chapter Learning Objective Questions

Answer the following questions in the space provided and check your answers on the page numbers listed.

| | |
|---|---|
| 2.1 | What is a neuron, and what are its three parts? p. 35 |

| | |
|---|---|
| 2.2 | What is a synapse? p. 36 |

| | |
|---|---|
| 2.3 | What is the action potential? p. 36 |

| | |
|---|---|
| 2.4 | What are neurotransmitters, and what role do they play in the transmission of signals from one neuron to another? p. 37 |

| | |
|---|---|
| 2.5 | What are some of the ways in which neurotransmitters affect our behaviour, and what are some of the major neurotransmitters? p. 38 |

| | |
|---|---|
| 2.6 | Why is an intact spinal cord important to normal functioning? p. 41 |

| | |
|---|---|
| 2.7 | What are the crucial functions handled by the brainstem? p. 41 |

| | |
|---|---|
| 2.8 | What are the primary functions of the cerebellum? p. 42 |

| | |
|---|---|
| 2.9 | What is the primary role of the thalamus? p. 43 |

| | |
|---|---|
| 2.10 | What are some of the processes regulated by the hypothalamus? p. 43 |

2.11 What is the role of the limbic system?  p. 43

2.12 What are the cerebral hemispheres, the cerebral cortex, and the corpus callosum? p. 44

2.13 What are some of the main areas within the frontal lobes, and what are their functions? p. 45–47

2.14 What are the primary functions of the parietal lobes in general and the somatosensory cortex in particular? p. 48

2.15 What are the primary functions of the occipital lobes in general and the primary visual cortex in particular? p. 48

2.16 What are major areas within the temporal lobes, and what are their functions? p. 48

2.17 What are the main functions of the left hemisphere? p. 50

2.18 What are the primary functions of the right hemisphere? p. 50

2.19 What is the significance of the split-brain operation? p. 51

2.20 What are some methods that have researchers used to learn about brain function? p. 53

2.21 What is the electroencephalo-gram (EEG), and what are three of the brain-wave patterns it reveals? p. 53

2.22 Does the brain stop changing at any point in development? p. 56

2.23 What must occur in the brain for there to be some recovery from brain damage? p. 56-57

2.24 What is the peripheral nervous system? p. 57

2.25 What are the roles of the sympathetic and parasympa-thetic nervous systems? p. 57–59

2.26 What is the endocrine system, and what are some of the glands within it? p. 59–60

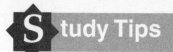 **S**tudy Tips

 **T**ry It

Learn to study more effectively and improve your memory with these tips and practical exercises.

## Memorizing Complex Information

There are memory techniques that make learning easier and faster. One technique, known as the "loci memory system," involves picturing yourself in a familiar setting and associating it with something you need to learn. Let's assume that you needed to memorize the function and structure of a neuron. Begin by picturing yourself walking into the entry hall of your home. At the same time pretend that you are walking through a dendrite. As you walk down the hall toward the living room, imagine that you are travelling in the dendrite to the cell body. As you exit the living room and walk down the hall toward the bedrooms, think of travelling down an axon toward the terminal button that contains the neurotransmitter. In this example you are connecting new information with something very familiar. We recall information much better when we involve our imagination. An even better way to perform this exercise would be to actually walk through your home while you visualize the parts of a neuron. In this situation you would not only be using your imagination but at the same time doing something physically. It is important to realize that we have strong memories for what we do physically. Just think how long you have remembered how to ride a bike even though you may not have ridden a bike for years.

## When and How to Study

1. Plan two hours of study time for every hour you spend in class.
2. Study difficult or boring subjects first.
3. Avoid long study sessions.
4. Be aware of your best time of day.
5. Use waiting time by studying flash cards.
6. Use a regular study area.
7. Don't get too comfortable.
8. Use a library.
9. Take frequent breaks.
10. Avoid noise distractions.

## Hanging Onto Money

Hold a five dollar bill by the end so it's hanging down. Place the thumb and index finger of your other hand around the centre of the bill about a quarter-inch away from it. Let go of the top end with the one hand and catch the bill with the other.

This time try it with a friend. Hold the bill the same way and tell your friend to catch the bill as soon as you let it go. Most of the time your friend will not catch it. Why is this more difficult for your friend?

*answer*

The difference is due to the speed of the nerve impulse. When your brain sends the instruction "Let go," it also sends at the same time the instruction "Catch." Your friend's experience involves more steps: 1) see the bill being let go, 2) send a message from the eyes to the back of the brain, 3) relay message to motor area, 4) send message from motor area to muscles.

Try this on people who have had a drink or two, to see how much alcohol slows their reaction time.

## *VangoNotes*

You can study on the go with *VangoNotes*. Simply download chapter reviews and listen to them on your MP3 player. Great for the gym, walking, or taking the bus. *VangoNotes* provide:

- *Big Ideas*: Your "need to know" for each chapter
- *Practice Tests*: A gut check for the Big Ideas to tell you if you need to keep studying
- *Key Terms*: Audio "flash cards" to help you review key concepts and terms
- *Rapid Review*: A quick drill session—use it right before your test

After studying the text and completing the Study Guide activities, answer these questions to determine if you need to review any areas before your exam.

1. The _____ is a specialized cell that transmits signals throughout the nervous system.
   a. neuron
   b. myelin
   c. glial cell
   d. neurotransmitter

2. The branch-like extensions of neurons that act as the primary receivers of signals from other neurons are the:
   a. myelin sheaths.
   b. axons.
   c. cell bodies.
   d. dendrites.

3. The junction where the axon of a sending neuron communicates with a receiving neuron is called the:
   a. reuptake site.
   b. receptor site.
   c. synapse.
   d. axon terminal.

4. A reversal of the electrical potential within a neuron that happens suddenly is called:
   a. a neural discharge.
   b. a refraction.
   c. refractory impulse.
   d. an action potential.

5. The "all-or-none" law of action potentials refers to:
   a. all the neurons in a nerve fire or none of them fire.
   b. all the dendrites must be activated before a neuron fires.
   c. all the axon terminals must be in refraction or the neuron does not fire.
   d. neurons either fire at full strength or not at all.

6. When a neurotransmitter that was previously released is taken back into the axon terminal intact and ready for use again, the process is known as:

   a. reassimilation.
   b. reduction.
   c. reuptake.
   d. synaptic transfer.

7. Neurons can conduct messages faster if they have:
   a. an axon with a myelin sheath.
   b. more than one cell body.
   c. a positive resting potential charge.
   d. fewer dendrites.

8. The _____ connects the brain with the peripheral nervous system.
   a. autonomic nervous system
   b. brainstem
   c. reticular formation
   d. spinal cord

9. All of the following are controlled by the medulla EXCEPT:
   a. heart rate.
   b. arousal.
   c. breathing.
   d. blood pressure.

10. Jamie can sleep through the loud party a neighbour is having but wakes up to the phone ringing because she is expecting a call. The _____ of her brain enables her to do this.
    a. medulla
    b. reticular formation
    c. thalamus
    d. pons

11. Which of the following regulates hunger, thirst, sexual behaviour, and many emotional experiences?
    a. thalamus
    b. amygdala
    c. hypothalamus
    d. hippocampus

12. According to the text, the part of the brain that makes us different from animals is the:

a. cerebral cortex.
b. thalamus.
c. limbic system.
d. cerebellum.

13. The two cerebral hemispheres are physically connected by a wide band of nerve fibres called the:
a. corpus callosum.
b. reticular formation.
c. amygdala.
d. nodes of Ranvier.

14. All of the following are lobes in the cerebral cortex EXCEPT the:
a. frontal lobe.
b. parietal lobe.
c. peripheral lobe.
d. temporal lobe.

15. As a consequence of damage to the right motor cortex, one might expect to have:
a. some loss of coordination on the right side of the body.
b. some loss of coordination on the left side of the body.
c. some loss of feeling on the right side of the body.
d. some loss of feeling on the left side of the body.

16. The term _____ refers to the loss or impairment of the ability to understand or communicate through writing or speaking.
a. language impairment syndrome
b. communication impairment syndrome
c. aphasia
d. agnosia

17. What area of the brain is important for planning?
a. thalamus
b. temporal lobe
c. cerebellum
d. frontal lobe

18. Which lobes of the cortex are primarily responsible for processing visual information?
a. occipital
b. parietal
c. temporal
d. frontal

19. Hearing is processed in:
a. the somatosensory cortex.
b. the primary auditory cortex.
c. Wernicke's area.
d. Broca's area.

20. For the majority of people what does their right hemisphere process?
a. speech
b. logic
c. recognition and expression of emotion
d. math

21. _____ brain waves are associated with deep relaxation.
a. Alpha
b. Beta
c. Delta
d. Theta

22. The CT scan and MRI are used to:
a. show the amount of activity in various parts of the brain.
b. measure electrical activity in the brain.
c. observe neural communication at synapses.
d. produce images of the structures within the brain.

23. Plasticity refers to:
a. the fissures of the cerebral cortex.
b. the neural condition within the axons of the cerebral hemispheres.
c. the brain's ability to reorganize and compensate for brain damage.
d. the appearance of areas of the brain that have been damaged.

24. The autonomic nervous system differs from the somatic nervous system in that its operation is largely:
a. involuntary.
b. voluntary.
c. controlled by the brain.
d. controlled by the spinal cord.

| Question Number | Answer | Learning Objective | Explanation for application questions |
|---|---|---|---|
| 1. | a. | 2.1 | The neuron is a specialized cell of the nervous system. |
| 2. | d. | 2.1 | |
| 3. | c. | 2.2 | |
| 4. | d. | 2.3 | The action potential is the reversal of the electrical potential within a neuron. |
| 5. | d. | 2.3 | |
| 6. | c. | 2.4 | |
| 7. | a. | 2.3 | Axons covered with the myelin sheath conduct the action potential more quickly than unmyelinated axons. |
| 8. | d. | 2.6 | |
| 9. | b. | 2.7 | The medulla controls life-sustaining, vital functions, such as heart rate, breathing, and maintaining blood pressure. |
| 10. | b. | 2.11 | Our reticular formation controls selective attention and arousal. |
| 11. | c. | 2.10 | |
| 12. | a. | 2.12 | Our higher functions of thinking, analysis, and integrating information are processed in our cerebral cortex. |
| 13. | a. | 2.12 | |
| 14. | c. | 2.12 | The cerebral cortex consists of the frontal, parietal, temporal, and occipital lobes. |
| 15. | b. | 2.18 | One side of the cerebral cortex controls the opposite side of the body. This is called contralateral. |
| 16. | c. | 2.24 | Aphasia is a disorder of understanding language or speaking. |
| 17. | d. | 2.13 | |
| 18. | a. | 2.15 | |
| 19. | b. | 2.16 | The primary auditory cortex processes hearing. |
| 20. | c. | 2.18 | |
| 21. | a. | 2.21 | |
| 22. | d. | 2.20 | CT scan and MRI show structures but not function of the brain. |
| 23. | c. | 2.23 | |
| 24. | a. | 2.24 | |

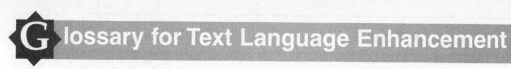

# Glossary for Text Language Enhancement

Students identified the following words from the text as needing more explanation. This page can be cut out, folded in half, and used as a bookmark for this chapter.

| term | definition |
|---|---|
| neurosurgeons | doctors who operate on the brain |
| neuroradiologists | doctors who x-ray the brain |
| plastic surgeons | doctors who repair physical appearance |
| anesthetists | doctors who use drugs to make people unconscious during operations |
| urologists | doctors who treat problems with the urinary and genital systems |
| cardiologists | doctors who take care of problems with the heart |
| surgical nurses | nurses who specialize in operating room skills |
| non-functional | not working |
| cerebral circulation | blood flow in the brain |
| propagating | reproducing |
| remarkably | impressive |
| seizures | shaking of muscles |
| regulate | control |
| sprouts | divides into branches |
| permeable | allows fluids to enter |
| fuse | put together as one |
| intact | whole |
| tremors | shaking |
| rigidity | not flexible |
| metabolism | ongoing process inside the body for digesting food and getting energy from it |
| bombarded | to receive a lot of information very quickly |
| jolt | a sudden bump or shock |
| influential | important and having a lot of control |
| abruptly | suddenly |
| prominent | important position or role |
| finely coordinated | small and smooth (as in movements) |
| cluster | group |
| impairment | problem with |
| site | location |
| trajectory | the path |
| sustains | receives; gets |
| partial vision | limited vision |
| bursts of sound | a lot of sound heard quickly |
| coherent | understandable |
| fluent | skilful in speech |

| term | definition |
|------|-----------|
| vague | not clear |
| bizarre | very strange |
| gibberish | words that make no sense |
| attentional deficits | unable to focus on one thing |
| idiomatic | the unique style of using words for a given language |
| sarcastically | a statement that means the opposite of what was said and is usually negative |
| simultaneously | happening at the same time |
| amplifies | increases |

# Thinking Critically

## Evaluation

Using your knowledge about how the human brain has been studied in the past and today, point out the advantages and the disadvantages of the older investigative methods: the case study, the autopsy, and the study of people with brain injuries or who have had brain surgery (including the split-brain operation). Follow the same procedure to discuss the more modern techniques: EEG, CT scan, PET scan, and fMRI.

## Point/Counterpoint

A continuing controversial issue is whether animals should be used in biopsychological research. Review the chapter and find each occasion in which animals were used to advance our knowledge of the brain. Using what you have read in this chapter and any other information you have acquired, prepare arguments to support each of the following positions:

a. The use of animals in research projects is ethical and justifiable because of the possible benefits to humankind.

b. The use of animals in research projects is not ethical or justifiable on the grounds of possible benefits to humankind.

## Psychology in Your Life

How would your life change if you had a massive stroke in your left hemisphere? How would it change if the stroke were in your right hemisphere? Which stroke would be more tragic for you, and why?

| | |
|---|---|
| neuron | neurotransmitter |
| cell body | receptors |
| dendrites | reuptake |
| axon | acetylcholine |
| synapse | dopamine |
| resting potential | norepinephrine |
| action potential | serotonin |

| | |
|---|---|
| Chemical that is released into synaptic cleft from axon terminal of sending neuron, crosses the synapse, and binds to appropriate receptor sites on the dendrites or cell body of receiving neuron. | A specialized cell that conducts impulses through the nervous system and contains three major parts—a cell body, dendrites, and an axon. |
| Sites on the dendrite or cell body of a neuron that will interact only with specific neurotransmitters. | The part of the neuron, containing the nucleus, that carries out the metabolic functions of the neuron. |
| The process by which neurotransmitters are taken from the synaptic cleft back into the axon terminal for later use. | The branchlike extensions of a neuron that receive signals from other neurons. |
| A neurotransmitter that plays a role in learning, memory, and rapid eye movement (REM) sleep and causes the skeletal muscle fibres to contract. | The slender, tail-like extension of the neuron that transmits signals to the dendrites or cell body of other neurons or to the muscles or glands. |
| A neurotransmitter that plays a role in learning, attention, and movement; a deficiency of dopamine is associated with Parkinson's disease, and an oversensitivity to it is associated with some cases of schizophrenia. | The junction where the axon of a sending neuron communicates with a receiving neuron across the synaptic cleft. |
| A neurotransmitter affecting eating and sleep; a deficiency of norepinephrine is associated with depression. | The membrane potential of a neuron at rest, about 70 millivolts. |
| A neurotransmitter that plays an important role in regulating mood, sleep, aggression, and appetite; a serotonin deficiency is associated with suicide, impulsive violence, and depression. | The sudden reversal of the resting potential, which initiates the firing of a neuron. |

| | |
|---|---|
| endorphins | reticular formation |
| myelin sheath | cerebellum |
| glial cells | thalamus |
| central nervous system | hypothalamus |
| spinal cord | limbic system |
| brainstem | cerebrum |
| medulla | cerebral hemispheres |

| | |
|---|---|
| A structure in the brainstem that plays a crucial role in arousal and attention and that screens sensory messages entering the brain. | Chemicals produced naturally by the brain that reduce pain and positively affect mood. |
| The brain structure that executes smooth, skilled body movements and regulates muscle tone and posture. | The white, fatty coating wrapped around some axons that acts as insulation and enables impulses to travel much faster. |
| The structure, located above the brainstem, that acts as a relay station for information flowing into or out of the higher brain centres. | Cells that help to make the brain more efficient by holding the neurons together, removing waste products, making the myelin coating, providing nutrients, and doing clean-up tasks. |
| A small but influential brain structure that controls the pituitary gland and regulates hunger, thirst, sexual behaviour, body temperature, and a wide variety of emotional behaviours. | The brain and the spinal cord |
| A group of structures in the brain, including the amygdala and hippocampus, that are collectively involved in emotion, memory, and motivation. | An extension of the brain, reaching from the base of the brain through the neck and spinal column, that transmits messages between the brain and the peripheral nervous system. |
| The largest structure of the human brain, consisting of two cerebral hemispheres connected by the corpus callosum and covered by the cerebral cortex. | The structure that begins at the point where the spinal cord enlarges as it enters the brain and that includes the medulla, the pons, and the reticular formation. |
| The right and left halves of the cerebrum, covered by the cerebral cortex and connected by the corpus callosum. | The part of the brainstem that controls heartbeat, blood pressure, breathing, coughing, and swallowing. |

| | |
|---|---|
| corpus callosum | aphasia |
| cerebral cortex | parietal lobes |
| association areas | somatosensory cortex |
| frontal lobes | occipital lobes |
| motor cortex | primary visual cortex |
| Broca's area | temporal lobes |
| Broca's aphasia | primary auditory cortex |

| | |
|---|---|
| A loss or impairment of the ability to understand or communicate through the written or spoken word, which results from damage to the brain pro-duction of speech sounds. | The thick band of nerve fibres that connects the two cerebral hemispheres and makes possible the transfer of information and the synchronization of activity between them. |
| The lobes that contain the somatosensory cortex and other areas that are responsible for body awareness and spatial orientation. | The grey, convoluted covering of the cerebral hemispheres that is responsi-ble for higher mental processes such as language, memory, and thinking. |
| The strip of tissue at the front of the parietal lobes where touch, pressure, temperature, and pain register in the cerebral cortex. | Areas of the cerebral cortex that house memories and are involved in thought, perception, learning, and language. |
| The lobes that contain the primary visual cortex, where vision registers, and association areas involved in the interpretation of visual information. | The lobes that control voluntary body movements, speech production, and such functions as thinking, motivation, planning for the future, impulse control, and emotional responses. |
| The area at the rear of the occipital lobes where vision registers in the cerebral cortex. | The strip of tissue at the rear of the frontal lobes that controls voluntary body movement. |
| The lobes that contain the primary auditory cortex, Wernicke's area, and association areas for interpreting auditory information. | The area in the frontal lobe, usually in the left hemisphere, that controls the ability to produce speech. |
| The part of the temporal lobes where hearing registers in the cerebral cortex. | An impairment in the ability physically to produce the speech sound; caused by damage to Broca's area. |

| | |
|---|---|
| Wernicke's aphasia | alpha wave |
| lateralization | delta wave |
| left hemisphere | microelectrode |
| right hemisphere | CT scan |
| split-brain operation | magnetic resonance imaging (MRI) |
| electroencephalo-gram | PET scan |
| beta wave | Wernicke's area |

| | |
|---|---|
| The brain wave associated with deep relaxation. | Aphasia resulting from damage to Wernicke's area, in which the patient's spoken language is fluent, but the content is either vague or incomprehensible to the listener. |
| The brain wave associated with slow-wave (deep) sleep. | The specialization of one of the cerebral hemispheres to handle a particular function. |
| An electrical wire so small that it can be used either to monitor the electrical activity of a single neuron or to stimulate activity within it. | The hemisphere that controls the right side of the body, coordinates complex movements, and, in 95 percent of people, controls the production of speech and written language. |
| A brain-scanning technique involving a rotating X-ray scanner and a high-speed computer analysis that produces slice-by-slice, cross-sectional images of the structure of the brain. | The hemisphere that controls the left side of the body and that, in most people, is specialized for visual-spatial perception and for interpreting non-verbal behaviour. |
| A diagnostic scanning technique that produces high-resolution images of the structures of the brain. | An operation, performed in severe cases of epilepsy, in which the corpus callosum is cut, separating the cerebral hemispheres and usually lessening the severity and frequency of grand mal seizures. |
| A brain-imaging technique that reveals activity in various parts of the brain, based on the amount of oxygen and glucose consumed. | A record of brain-wave activity made by the electroencephalograph. |
| The language area in the temporal lobe involved in comprehension of the spoken word and in formulation of coherent speech and written language. | The brain wave associated with mental or physical activity. |

| | |
|---|---|
| plasticity | adrenal glands |
| peripheral nervous system | amygdala |
| sympathetic nervous system | hippocampus |
| parasympathetic nervous system | theta wave |
| endocrine system | |
| hormone | |
| pituitary gland | |

| | |
|---|---|
| A pair of endocrine glands that release hormones that prepare the body for emergencies and stressful situations and also release small amounts of the sex hormones. | The ability of the brain to reorganize and compensate for brain damage. |
| A structure in the limbic system that plays an important role in emotion, particularly in response to aversive stimuli. | The nerves connecting the central nervous system to the rest of the body. |
| A structure in the limbic system that plays a central role in the formation of long-term memories. | The division of the autonomic nervous system that mobilizes the body's resources during stress, emergencies, or heavy exertion, preparing the body for action. |
| A slow brain wave that occurs during light sleep, trances, and the state just before deep sleep or just before wakening. | The division of the autonomic nervous system that is associated with relaxation and the conservation of energy and that brings the heightened bodily responses back to normal following an emergency. |
| | A system of ductless glands in various parts of the body that manufacture and secrete hormones into the bloodstream or lymph fluids, thus affecting cells in other parts of the body. |
| | A substance manufactured and released in one part of the body that affects other parts of the body. |
| | The endocrine gland located in the brain and often called the "master gland," which releases hormones that control other endocrine glands and also releases a growth hormone. |

# 3

# SENSATION AND PERCEPTION

| Module 3.2 Vision | 1. Light: What We See |
| | |
| | 2. The Eye: Window to the Visual Sensory World |
| | 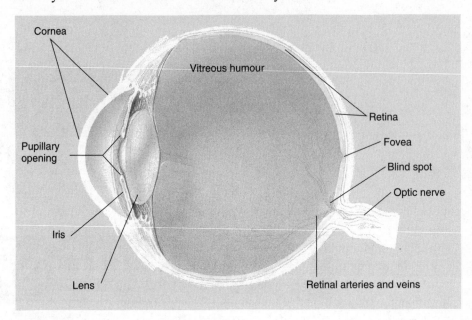 |
| | 3. Colour Vision: A Multicoloured World |

| Module 3.3 Hearing | 1. Sound: What We Hear |
| | 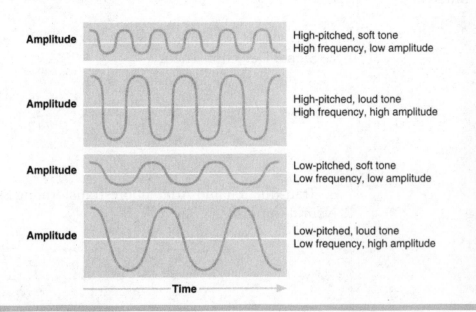 |

2. The Ear: More to It Than Meets the Eye

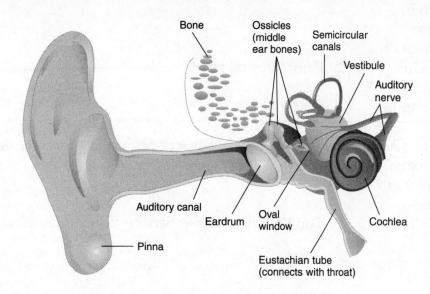

3. Theories of Hearing: How Hearing Works

4. Hearing Loss: Kinds and Causes

| | |
|---|---|
| Module 3.4<br>Smell and<br>Taste | 1. Smell: Sensing Scents |

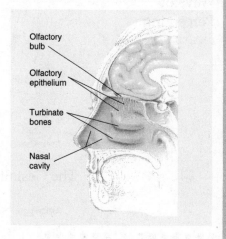

2. Taste: What the Tongue Can Tell

| | |
|---|---|
| Module 3.5<br>The Skin<br>Senses:<br>Information<br>from Our<br>Natural<br>Clothing | 1. The Mechanism of Touch: How Touch Works<br><br>2. Pain: Physical Hurts |
| Module 3.6<br>The Spatial<br>Orientation<br>Senses | 1. The Kinesthetic Sense: Keeping Track of Our Body Parts<br><br>2. The Vestibular Sense: Sensing Up and Down and Changes in Speed |

Cochlea

Semicircular canals

Vestibular sacs

| | |
|---|---|
| Module 3.7<br>Perception:<br>Ways of<br>Perceiving | **Reversing Figure and Ground**<br><br>1. The Gestalt Principles of Perceptual Organization |

A     B
**(a) Similarity**    **(b) Proximity**    **(c) Continuity**    **(d) Closure**

2. Perceptual Constancy

3. Depth Perception: Perceiving What's Up Close and What's Far Away

4. Extraordinary Perceptions

    a. Ambiguous Figures
    b. Impossible Figures
    c. Illusions

**The Three-Pronged Trident**
This is an impossible figure because the middle prong appears to be in two places at the same time.

| | |
|---|---|
| Module 3.8 Additional Influences on Perception | 1. Bottom-Up and Top-Down Processing |
| | 2. Perceptual Set |
| | 3. Subliminal Persuasion: Does It Work? |
| Apply It! | **Noise and Hearing Loss: Bad Vibrations** |
| | 1. Noisy Toys |
| | 2. Fireworks |
| | 3. Amplified music |
| | 4. Power Tools |

# Chapter Learning Objective Questions

Answer the following questions in the space provided and check your answers on the page numbers listed.

3.1  What is the difference between sensation and perception? p. 70

3.2  What is the difference between the absolute threshold and the difference threshold? p. 70

3.3  How are sensory stimuli in the environment experienced as sensations? p. 72

3.4  How do the cornea, the iris, and the pupil function in vision? p. 73

3.5  What are the lens and the retina? p. 74

3.6  What roles do the rods and cones play in vision? p. 75

3.7  What path does the neural impulse take from the retina to the visual cortex? p. 76

3.8  What are the three dimensions that combine to provide the colours we experience? p. 77

3.9  What two major theories attempt to explain colour vision? p. 77

3.10 What determines the pitch and the loudness of sound, and how is each quality measured? p. 80

| | |
|---|---|
| 3.11 How do the outer, middle, and inner ears function in hearing? p. 82 | |
| 3.12 What two major theories attempt to explain hearing? p. 82–83 | |
| 3.13 What are some major causes of hearing loss? p. 83 | |
| 3.14 What path does a smell message take on its journey from the nose to the brain? p. 84 | |
| 3.15 What are the five primary taste sensations, and how are they detected? p. 85 | |
| 3.16 How does the skin provide sensory information? p. 87 | |
| 3.17 What beneficial purpose does pain serve? p. 88 | |
| 3.18 What is the gate-control theory of pain? p. 88 | |
| 3.19 What are endorphins? p. 88 | |
| 3.20 What kind of information does the kinesthetic sense provide, and how is this sensory information detected? p. 89 | |

3.21 What is the vestibular sense, and where are its sensory receptors located? p. 90

3.22 What are the Gestalt principles of perceptual organization? p. 91

3.23 What is perceptual constancy, and what are its four types? p. 92

3.24 What are the binocular depth cues? p. 93

3.25 What are seven monocular depth cues? p. 94

3.26 In what types of situations do we rely more on bottom-up or top-down processing? p. 98

3.27 How does perceptual set affect our experience of reality? p. 99

Learn to study more effectively and improve your memory with these tips and practical exercises.

## Study in Groups

Research has shown that one of the most effective ways to learn is to study with other students. Your grades on exams will be better and you will have a lot more fun doing it!

### How to Form a Group

1. Look for dedicated students who share some of your academic goals and challenges.

2. You could write a note on the blackboard asking interested students to contact you, or pass around a sign-up sheet before class.

3. Limit groups to five or six people.

4. Test the group by planning a one-time-only session. If that session works, plan another.

## Possible Activities for a Study Group

1. Compare notes.

2. Have discussions and debates about the material.

3. Test each other with questions brought to the group meeting by each member.

4. Practise teaching each other.

5. Brainstorm possible test questions.

6. Share suggestions for problems in the areas of finances, transportation, child care, time scheduling, or other barriers.

7. Develop a plan at the beginning of each meeting from the list above or any ideas you have.

## What Do You Perceive?

Do these steps go on continuously?

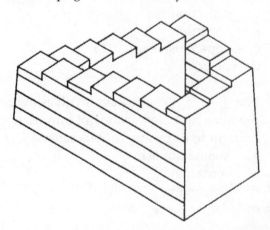

In the figure below, which long lines are parallel?

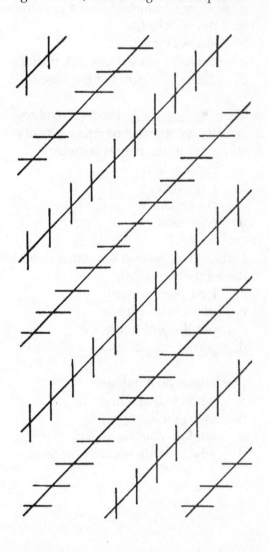

After studying the text and completing the Study Guide activities, answer these questions to determine if you need to review any areas before your exam.

1. The detection of sensory stimuli and transmission back to the brain is called:
   a. sensation.
   b. reception.
   c. consciousness.
   d. perception.

2. The _____ process involves interpretation and organization of information brought to us by our various senses.
   a. somnambulism
   b. sensation
   c. perception
   d. convergence

3. Absolute threshold is the minimum amount of sensory stimulation that a person can:
   a. never detect.
   b. always detect.
   c. detect in at least one in ten trials.
   d. detect 50 percent of the time.

4. The _____ process involves sensory receptors converting sensory stimulation into neural impulses.
   a. sublimation
   b. transduction
   c. convergence
   d. refraction

5. Light moves toward the retina in which of the following paths?
   a. lens, cornea, pupil
   b. pupil, lens, cornea
   c. pupil, cornea, lens
   d. cornea, pupil, lens

6. Our pupils do not dilate:
   a. when telling a lie.
   b. in bright light.
   c. while becoming angry.
   d. when we are sexually aroused.

7. All of the following are true of cones EXCEPT:
   a. They play a key role in colour vision.
   b. They are critical in our ability to notice fine detail.
   c. They function best in bright light.
   d. They are more numerous than rods.

8. Which of the following sets of colours are the three types of cones particularly sensitive to?
   a. yellow, red, and blue
   b. red, white, and blue
   c. green, blue, and yellow
   d. red, green, and blue

9. After leaving each eye, the optic nerves come together at a point:
   a. where the information is interpreted by the brain.
   b. where information from each eye is combined into one impulse.
   c. deep in the pons.
   d. where some of the nerve fibres cross to the opposite side of the brain.

10. Saturation refers to the:
    a. intensity of the colour we view.
    b. brightness of the colour we view.
    c. purity of the colour we view.
    d. wavelength of the colour we view.

11. Which of the following statements is NOT true of the amplitude of sound?
    a. It is measured in decibels.
    b. It is mainly the pitch of the sound.
    c. It depends on the magnitude of a sound wave.
    d. It depends on the energy of a sound wave.

12. Which of the following is not a name of one of the bones in the middle ear?
    a. mallet
    b. anvil
    c. hammer
    d. stirrup

13. The hair cells are contained:
    a. within the auditory nerve.
    b. along the inner membrane of the eardrum.
    c. in the tiny bones of the inner ear.
    d. within the cochlea.

14. When you listen to a recording of your own voice, what is the main reason that it sounds so odd to you?
    a. You typically do not pay attention to your own voice.
    b. You are being too self-conscious.
    c. You are hearing it without bone conduction.
    d. Recording equipment greatly distorts the human voice.

15. Place theory and frequency theory are two explanations of:
    a. colour blindness.
    b. sound localization.
    c. auditory threshold shift.
    d. pitch perception.

16. Conductive hearing loss can be caused by:
    a. injury to the eardrum or ossicles.
    b. injury to the hair cells and auditory nerve.
    c. injury to the auditory nerve or semicircular canals.
    d. injury to the semicircular canals and the ossicles.

17. _____ probably plays the biggest role in nerve deafness.
    a. Lifelong exposure to excessive noise
    b. Disease
    c. Birth defects
    d. Aging

18. Hearing aids are not useful if the damage is to the:
    a. cochlea.
    b. anvil.
    c. pistole.
    d. auditory nerve.

19. The largest sense organ is sensitive to:
    a. chemical concentration.
    b. touch.
    c. sound.
    d. light.

20. The _____ theory suggests that nerve fibres carrying messages that pressure is being applied to some part of the body can prevent messages from getting through to the brain.
    a. gate-control theory
    b. opponent-process theory
    c. volley principle
    d. Gestalt principle

21. What causes "runner's high"?
    a. naloxone
    b. endorphins
    c. placebo
    d. epinephrine

22. Information about the position of body parts and about body movement, detected by receptors in the muscles, ligaments, and joints, is referred to as:
    a. the vestibular sense.
    b. the gustatory sense.
    c. the tactile sense.
    d. the kinesthetic sense.

23. The vestibular sense:
    a. integrates sensations from the chemical senses.
    b. monitors the internal organs of the body.
    c. provides information about the position of body parts.
    d. provides information about movement and our orientation in space.

24. The most fundamental principle of perceptual organization is called the:
    a. figure-ground relationship.
    b. volley principle.
    c. monocular phenomenon.
    d. law of closure.

25. The tendency to perceive objects as maintaining the same size, shape, and brightness despite differences in distance, viewing angle, and lighting is called perceptual:
    a. organization.
    b. rigidity.
    c. adaptation.
    d. constancy.

# Answers to Multiple-Choice Questions

| Question Number | Answer | Learning Objective | Explanation for application questions |
|---|---|---|---|
| 1. | a. | 3.1 | Sensation is the process of "taking in" sensory information. |
| 2. | c. | 3.1 | Perception is the process of "interpreting" sensory information. |
| 3. | d. | 3.2 | |
| 4. | b. | 3.3 | |
| 5. | d. | 3.4 | Light goes through the cornea and the pupil, and then strikes the retina. |
| 6. | b. | 3.4 | Our pupil constricts in bright light to protect the eye from damage. |
| 7. | d. | 3.6 | There are many more rods than cones. |
| 8. | d. | 3.6 | |
| 9. | a. | 3.7 | |
| 10. | c. | 3.8 | |
| 11. | b. | 3.10 | |
| 12. | a. | 3.11 | The middle ear's bones are the anvil, hammer, and stirrup. |
| 13. | d. | 3.11 | Hair cells are on the basilar membrane in the cochlea. |
| 14. | c. | 3.12 | |
| 15. | d. | 3.12 | |
| 16. | a. | 3.13 | Conductive hearing loss may be caused by loud noise. |
| 17. | a | 3.13 | |
| 18. | d. | 3.13 | |
| 19. | b. | 3.16 | Skin is our largest sense organ. |
| 20. | a. | 3.18 | |
| 21. | b. | 3.19 | Endorphins are chemicals made in the brain that result in pain reduction and a feeling of euphoria. |
| 22. | d. | 3.20 | |
| 23. | d. | 3.21 | |
| 24. | a. | 3.22 | |
| 25. | d. | 3.23 | |

# **G**lossary for Text Language Enhancement

Students identified the following words from the text as needing more explanation. This page can be cut out, folded in half, and used as a bookmark for this chapter.

| term | definition |
| --- | --- |
| transmit | send |
| rudimentary | simple; not fully developed |
| fundamental | basic element or part |
| scant | little or few |
| dimmest | lowest |
| arbitrarily | based on one's preference |
| vintage | a particular type, or year |
| scan a sea of faces | look at many people's faces |
| diminish | reduce |
| circular | round |
| subtle | hardly noticeable |
| dilate | open up to be larger |
| suspended | hanging |
| composed of | made up of |
| transparent | able to see through |
| correctable | can be fixed |
| decreases sharply | decreases quickly |
| encode | change into |
| occupied | filled |
| adapt | make changes |
| absorbed | taken in |
| defects | problems |
| dispel | to drive away |
| distinguish | to tell the difference between |
| pulsating | to beat or throb |
| flute | a musical instrument in which air is blown into the mouthpiece |
| oddly shaped | not the usual shape |
| synchronized | working together |
| endure | having to put up with something, usually not nice |
| noxious fumes | harmful gas |
| inhalant | used to breathe in medicine |
| cluster | group together |
| crevice | a narrow crack or split |
| depresses the skin | pushes in on the skin |
| persists | continues |
| coursing | flowing |
| literal | using the most common meaning of the word |
| converge | come together |

| term | definition |
|------|------------|
| ambiguous<br>overhead<br>to decipher | not clear meaning<br>above us<br>to figure out; understand |

## Thinking Critically

### Evaluation

Using what you have learned about the factors that contribute to hearing loss, prepare a statement indicating what the government should do to control noise pollution, even to the extent of banning certain noise hazards. Consider the workplace, the home, toys, machinery, rock concerts, and so on.

### Point/Counterpoint

Much commercial advertising is aimed at providing products that reduce or eliminate pain. Prepare a sound, logical argument supporting one of the following positions:

a. Pain is valuable and necessary.

b. Pain is not necessary.

### Psychology in Your Life

Vision and hearing are generally believed to be the two most highly prized senses. How would your life change if you lost your sight? How would your life change if you lost your hearing? Which sense would you find more traumatic to lose? Why?

| | |
|---|---|
| sensation | sensory receptors |
| perception | transduction |
| absolute threshold | sensory adaptation |
| difference threshold | visible spectrum |
| just noticeable difference | cornea |
| Weber's law | lens |
| signal detection theory | accommodation |

| | |
|---|---|
| Specialized cells in each sense organ that detect and respond to sensory stimuli—light, sound, odours, etc.—and transduce (convert) the stimuli into neural impulses. | The process through which the senses pick up visual, auditory, and other sensory stimuli and transmit them to the brain; sensory information that has registered in the brain but has not been interpreted. |
| The process by which sensory receptors convert sensory stimulation— light, sound, odours, etc.—into neural impulses. | The process by which sensory information is actively organized and interpreted by the brain. |
| The process of becoming less sensitive to an unchanging sensory stimulus over time. | The minimum amount of sensory stimulation that can be detected 50 percent of the time. |
| The narrow band of electromagnetic rays that are visible to the human eye. | The smallest increase or decrease in a physical stimulus required to produce a difference in sensation that is noticeable 50 percent of the time. |
| The transparent covering of the coloured part of the eye that bends light rays inward through the pupil. | The smallest change in sensation that we are able to detect 50 percent of the time. |
| The transparent structure behind the iris that changes in shape as it focuses images on the retina. | The law stating that the just noticeable difference for all our senses depends on the proportion or percentage of change in a stimulus rather than on a fixed amount of change. |
| The changing in shape of the lens as it focuses objects on the retina, becoming more spherical for near objects and flatter for far objects. | The view that detection of a sensory stimulus involves both discriminating a stimulus from background "noise" and deciding whether the stimulus is actually present. |

| | |
|---|---|
| rods | subliminal persuasion |
| cones | hue |
| fovea | saturation |
| opponent-process theory | brightness |
| afterimage | colour blindness |
| subliminal perception | frequency |
| optic nerve | amplitude |

| | |
|---|---|
| Sending persuasive messages below the recipient's level of awareness. | The light-sensitive receptors in the retina that provide vision in dim light in black, white, and shades of grey. |
| The property of light commonly referred to as colour (red, blue, green, etc.), determined primarily by the wavelength of light reflected from a surface. | The receptor cells in the retina that enable us to see colour and fine detail in adequate light, but that do not function in dim light. |
| The degree to which light waves producing a colour are of the same wavelength; the purity of a colour. | A small area of the retina, 1/50 of an inch in diameter, that provides the clearest and sharpest vision because it has the largest concentration of cones. |
| The dimension of visual sensation that is dependent on the intensity of light reflected from a surface and that corresponds to the amplitude of the light wave. | The theory that certain cells in the visual system increase their firing rate to signal one colour and decrease their firing rate to signal the opposing colour (red/green, yellow/blue, white/black). |
| The inability to distinguish some or all colours in vision, resulting from a defect in the cones. | The visual sensation that remains after a stimulus is withdrawn. |
| Measured in the unit hertz, the number of sound waves or cycles per second, determining the pitch of the sound. | Perceiving sensory stimulation that is below the absolute threshold. |
| Measured in decibels, the magnitude or intensity of a sound wave, determining the loudness of the sound; in vision the *amplitude* of a light wave affects the brightness of a stimulus. | The nerve that carries visual information from the retina to the brain. |

| | |
|---|---|
| decibel | hair cells |
| timbre | place theory |
| audition | frequency theory |
| outer ear | flavour |
| middle ear | olfaction |
| inner ear | olfactory epithelium |
| cochlea | olfactory bulbs |

| | |
|---|---|
| Sensory receptors for hearing, found in the cochlea. | A unit of measurement of the intensity or loudness of sound based on the amplitude of the sound wave. |
| The theory that sounds of different frequency or pitch cause maximum activation of hair cells at certain locations along the basilar membrane. | The distinctive quality of a sound that distinguishes it from other sounds of the same pitch and loudness. |
| The theory that hair cell receptors vibrate the same number of times as the sounds that reach them, thereby accounting for how variations in pitch are transmitted to the brain. | The sensation of hearing; the process of hearing. |
| The combined sensory experience of taste, smell, and touch. | The visible part of the ear, consisting of the pinna and the auditory canal. |
| The sensation of smell; the process of smell. | The portion of the ear containing the ossicles, which connect the eardrum to the oval window and amplify the vibrations as they travel to the inner ear. |
| A patch of tissue at the top of the nasal cavity that contains about 10 million receptors for smell. | The innermost portion of the ear, containing the cochlea, the vestibular sacs, and the semicircular canals. |
| Two matchstick-sized structures above the nasal cavities, where smell sensations first register in the brain. | The snail-shaped, fluid-filled organ in the inner ear that contains the hair cells (the sound receptors). |

| | |
|---|---|
| gustation | vestibular sense |
| taste buds | semicircular canals |
| tactile | Gestalt |
| gate-control theory | figure-ground |
| endorphins | innate |
| perceptual set | perceptual constancy |
| kinesthetic sense | size constancy |

| | |
|---|---|
| Sense that provides information about movement and our orientation in space through sensory receptors in the semicircular canals and vestibular sacs, which detect changes in the movement/orientation of the head. | The sensation of taste. |
| Three fluid-filled tubular canals in the inner ear that provide information about rotating head movements. | The structures that are composed of 60 to 100 sensory receptors for taste. |
| A German word roughly meaning "form" or "pattern." | Pertaining to the sense of touch. |
| A principle of perceptual organization whereby the visual field is perceived in terms of an object (figure) standing out against a background (ground). | The theory that the pain signals transmitted by slow-firing nerve fibres can be blocked at the spinal gate if fast-firing fibres get their message to the gate first, or if the brain itself inhibits transmission of the pain messages. |
| Inborn, unlearned. | Chemicals, produced naturally by the pituitary gland, that reduce pain and positively affect mood. |
| The tendency to perceive objects as maintaining stable properties, such as size, shape, brightness, and colour, despite differences in distance, viewing angle, and lighting. | An example of top-down processing where individuals' expectations affect their perceptions. |
| The tendency to perceive objects as the same size regardless of changes in the retinal image. | The sense providing information about relative position and movement of body parts. |

| | |
|---|---|
| retinal image | binocular disparity |
| shape constancy | monocular depth cues |
| brightness constancy | feature detectors |
| colour constancy | pheromones |
| depth perception | illusion |
| binocular depth cues | bottom-up processing |
| convergence | top-down processing |
| trichromatic theory | retina |

| | |
|---|---|
| A binocular depth cue resulting from differences between the two retinal images cast by objects at distances up to about six metres. | The image of objects in the visual field projected onto the retina. |
| Depth cues that can be perceived by only one eye. | The tendency to perceive objects as having a stable or unchanging shape regardless of differences in viewing angle. |
| Neurons in the brain that respond only to specific visual patterns (e.g., lines or angles). | The tendency to see objects as maintaining the same brightness regardless of differences in lighting conditions. |
| Chemicals excreted by humans and other animals that act as signals to, and patterns of, behaviour from members of the same species. | The tendency to see objects as maintaining about the same colour regardless of differences in lighting conditions. |
| A false perception of actual stimuli involving a misperception of size, shape, or the relationship of one element to another. | The ability to see in three dimensions and to estimate distance. |
| Information processing in which individual components or bits of data are combined until a complete perception is formed. | Depth cues that depend on two eyes working together; convergence and binocular disparity. |
| Application of previous experience and conceptual knowledge to first recognize the whole of a perception and thus easily identify the simpler elements of that whole. | A binocular depth cue in which the eyes turn inward as they focus on nearby objects—the closer an object, the greater the convergence. |
| The tissue at the back of the eye that contains the rods and the cones and onto which the retinal image is projected. | The theory of colour vision suggesting that there are three types of cones, which are maximally sensitive to red, green, or blue, and that varying levels of activity in these receptors can produce all of the colours. |

# 4

## STATES OF CONSCIOUSNESS

### C H A P T E R   O U T L I N E

This outline provides a way to organize your notes from both the text and the lecture. It will also serve as a review for the exam.

| | |
|---|---|
| Module 4.1 Circadian Rhythms: Our 24-Hour Highs and Lows | 1. The Suprachiasmatic Nucleus: The Body's Timekeeper<br><br>2. Jet Lag: Where Am I and What Time Is It?<br><br>3. Shift Work: Working Day and Night |

| | |
|---|---|
| Module 4.2 Sleep: That Mysterious One-Third of Our Lives | 1. NREM and REM Sleep: Watching the Eyes |
| | 2. Sleep Cycles: The Nightly Pattern of Sleep |

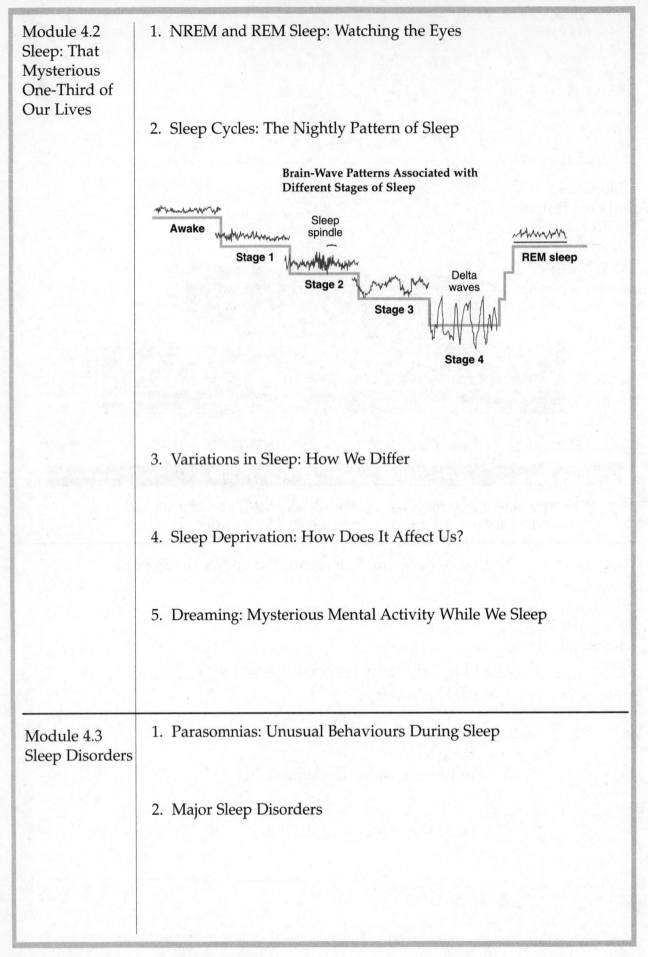

**Brain-Wave Patterns Associated with Different Stages of Sleep**

Awake

Sleep spindle

Stage 1

Stage 2

Delta waves

Stage 3

REM sleep

Stage 4

| | |
|---|---|
| | 3. Variations in Sleep: How We Differ |
| | 4. Sleep Deprivation: How Does It Affect Us? |
| | 5. Dreaming: Mysterious Mental Activity While We Sleep |
| Module 4.3 Sleep Disorders | 1. Parasomnias: Unusual Behaviours During Sleep |
| | 2. Major Sleep Disorders |

**C**hapter Learning Objective Questions

Answer the following questions in the space provided and check your answers on the page numbers listed.

| | |
|---|---|
| 4.1 What is a circadian rhythm, and which rhythms are most relevant to the study of sleep? p. 109 | |
| 4.2 What is the suprachiasmatic nucleus? p. 109 | |
| 4.3 What are some problems experienced by employees who work rotating shifts? p. 110 | |
| 4.4 How does a sleeper act physically during NREM sleep? p. 111 | |
| 4.5 How does the body respond physically during REM sleep? p. 112 | |
| 4.6 What is the progression of NREM stages and REM sleep that a person goes through in a typical night of sleep? p. 113 | |
| 4.7 How do sleep patterns change over the lifespan? p. 114 | |
| 4.8 What factors influence our sleep needs? p. 114 | |
| 4.9 What happens when people are deprived of REM sleep? What function does REM sleep appear to serve? p. 115 | |
| | |

**4.10** How do REM and NREM dreams differ? p. 115

**4.11** In general, what have researchers found regarding the content of dreams? p. 116

**4.12** What are the characteristics common to sleepwalking and sleep terrors? p. 119

**4.13** What is a sleep terror? p. 119

**4.14** How do nightmares differ from sleep terrors? p. 119

**4.15** What are the major symptoms of narcolepsy? p. 120

**4.16** What is sleep apnea? p. 120

**4.17** What is insomnia? p. 120

**4.18** For what purposes is meditation used? p. 121

**4.19** What is hypnosis, and when is it most useful? p. 122

4.20 What is the difference between physical and psychological drug dependence? p. 124

4.21 How do stimulants affect the user? p. 125

4.22 What effects do amphetamines have on the user? p. 125

4.23 How does cocaine affect the user? p. 125

4.24 What are the main effects of hallucinogens, and what are three psychoactive drugs in this class? p. 126

4.25 What are some harmful effects associated with heavy marijuana use? p. 126

4.26 What are some of the effects of depressants, and what drugs make up this category? p. 128

4.27 What are the general effects of narcotics, and what are several drugs in this category? p. 128

4.28 What are some of the causes of insomnia and what can we do to battle it? p. 131

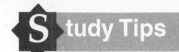

# S tudy Tips          # T ry It

Learn to study more effectively and improve your memory with these tips and practical exercises.

## Better Test Taking

1. Predict the test questions. Ask your instructor to describe the test format—how long it will be, and what kind of questions to expect (essay, multiple choice, problems, etc.).

2. Have a section in your notebook labelled "Test Questions" and add several questions to this section after every lecture and after reading the text. Record topics instructors repeat several times or go back to in subsequent lectures. Write down questions the instructor poses to students.

3. Arrive early so you can do a relaxation exercise. (There's one in Chapter 4 of our textbook.)

4. Ask about the procedure for asking questions during the test.

5. Know the rules for taking the test so you do not create the impression of cheating.

6. Scan the whole test immediately. Budget your time based on how many points each section is worth.

7. Read the directions slowly. Then reread them.

8. Answer the easiest, shortest questions first. This gives you the experience of success and stimulates associations. This prepares your mind for more difficult questions.

9. Next, answer multiple-choice, true-false, and fill-in-the-blank questions.

10. Use memory techniques when you're stuck.
    • If your recall on something is blocked, remember something else that's related.
    • Start from the general and go to the specific.

11. Look for answers in other test questions. A term, name, date, or other fact that you can't remember might appear in the test itself.

12. Don't change an answer unless you are sure because your first instinct is usually best.

(See Study Tips Chapter 5 for more test-taking hints.)

## Relaxing through Meditation

Find a quiet place and sit in a comfortable position.

1. Close your eyes.

2. Relax all your muscles deeply. Begin with your feet and move slowly upward, relaxing the muscles in your legs, buttocks, abdomen, chest, shoulders, neck, and finally your face. Allow your whole body to remain in this deeply relaxed state.

3. Now concentrate on your breathing, and breathe in and out through your nose. Each time you breathe out, silently say the word om to yourself.

4. Repeat this process for 20 minutes. (You can open your eyes to look at your watch periodically, but don't use an alarm.) When you are finished, remain seated for a few minutes— first with your eyes closed, and then with them open.

Benson recommends that you maintain a passive attitude. Don't try to force yourself to relax. Just let it happen. If a distracting thought comes to mind, ignore it and just repeat om each time you exhale. It is best to practise this exercise once or twice each day, but not within two hours of your last meal. Digestion interferes with the relaxation response.

## Battling Insomia: Hints for a Better Night's Sleep

Sleep is vital to your waking life, including energy and mental alertness. Empirical research (Murtagh & Greenwood, 1995) has indicated that there are things you can do to help you get a good night's sleep.

1. **Use your bed only for sleep.** Don't read, study, write letters, watch TV, eat, or talk on the phone on your bed.

2. **Leave the bedroom whenever you cannot fall sleep** after 10 minutes. Go to another room and read, watch television, or listen to music. Don't return to bed for another try

until you feel more tired. Repeat the process as many times as necessary until you fall asleep within 10 minutes.

3. **Establish a consistent, relaxing ritual** to follow each night just before bedtime. For example, take a warm bath, eat a small snack, brush your teeth, pick out your clothes for the next day, and so on.

4. **Set your alarm and wake up at the same time every day**, including weekends, regardless of how much you have slept. No naps are allowed during the day.

5. **Exercise regularly**—but not within several hours of bedtime. (Exercise raises body temperature and makes it more difficult to fall asleep.)

6. **Establish regular mealtimes**. Don't eat heavy or spicy meals close to bedtime. If you must eat, try milk and a few crackers.

7. **Beware of caffeine and nicotine**—they are sleep disturbers. Avoid caffeine within six hours and smoking within one or two hours of bedtime.

8. **Avoid wrestling with your problems when you go to bed**. Try counting backward from 1000 by twos; or try a progressive relaxation exercise.

## Using Your Dreams

History is full of cases where dreams have been a pathway to creativity and discovery. Otto Loewi, a pharmacologist, had spent years studying the chemical transmission of nerve impulses. A tremendous breakthrough in his research came when he dreamed of an experiment three nights in a row. The first two nights he woke up and scribbled the experiment on paper. But the next morning, he couldn't tell what the notes meant. On the third night, he got up after having the dream. This time, instead of making notes he went straight to his laboratory and performed the experiment. Loewi later said that if the experiment had occurred to him while awake he would have rejected it, but instead he won the Nobel Prize!

Being able to take advantage of dreams for problem solving is improved if you think intently about a problem before you go to bed. State the problem clearly and review all important information.

## How to Remember Your Dreams

1. Keep a pen and paper or tape recorder beside your bed and plan to remember your dreams.

2. If possible try to awaken gradually without an alarm. Natural awakening is almost always soon after a REM period.

3. If you rarely remember your dreams, you may want to set an alarm clock for one hour before you usually get up. Although not as effective as waking up naturally, this method may help you remember a dream.

4. When you wake up, lie still and review the dream images with your eyes closed. Try to recall as many details as possible.

5. If you can, make your first dream notes (written or taped) with your eyes still closed. Describe feelings, plot, characters, and actions of the dream.

6. Review the dream again and record as many additional details as you can remember. Dream memories disappear quickly.

7. Keep a diary and review it periodically, which will reveal recurrent themes, conflicts, and emotions. This often produces insights.

After studying the text and completing the Study Guide activities, answer these questions to determine if you need to review any areas before your exam.

1. During REM sleep, brain activity _____ while body movements _____.
   a. decreases; increase
   b. increases; decrease
   c. increases; are the same as in NREM sleep
   d. is the same as in NREM sleep; decrease

2. _____ dreams have a narrative or dreamlike quality and are more visual, vivid, emotional, and peculiar than _____ dreams, which characteristically are cognitive (i.e., resembling thought).
   a. NREM; ordinary
   b. lucid; REM
   c. REM; NREM
   d. symbolic; telepathic

3. Circadian rhythms are the regular fluctuations from high to low points of certain bodily functions that occur over the course of:
   a. a day.
   b. an hour.
   c. a week.
   d. a month or longer.

4. The internal biological clock seems to operate on a _____ hour day when external cues are eliminated.
   a. 21
   b. 23
   c. 25
   d. 27

5. The main reason for jet lag is that:
   a. travellers lose a night's sleep.
   b. the traveller's internal biological clock is no longer synchronized with clock time.
   c. airline travel disrupts body temperature.
   d. jet travel temporarily disrupts the suprachiasmatic nucleus.

6. Which of the following is NOT characteristic of people who work rotating shifts?
   a. disturbed sleep
   b. digestive problems

   c. greater efficiency and alertness during subjective night
   d. increased tendency to use caffeine, alcohol, and sleeping pills

7. Research suggests that rotating work schedules from days to evenings to nights and changing work schedules every three weeks rather than every week results in:
   a. more health problems.
   b. no change in worker productivity.
   c. high personnel turnover.
   d. higher work satisfaction.

8. Which of the following is NOT characteristic of REM sleep?
   a. paralysis of large muscles
   b. dreaming
   c. delta waves
   d. increase in blood pressure, heart rate, and respiration

9. The average length of a sleep cycle in adults is:
   a. 30 minutes.
   b. 60 minutes.
   c. 90 minutes.
   d. 120 minutes.

10. How many sleep cycles does the average person have each night?
    a. one
    b. three
    c. five
    d. seven

11. Bruce will be 75 years old in several months. Which of the following would be true of his sleep if he is typical of aging adults?
    a. He will have more awakenings and less deep sleep.
    b. He will have deeper sleep with fewer dreams.
    c. He will sleep longer than he did when he was 40.
    d. He will be more able to sleep anywhere.

12. Which age group is usually sleepy during the day regardless of the amount of sleep at night?
    a. infants
    b. children from age six to puberty
    c. adolescents
    d. the elderly

13. When comparing larks to owls:
    a. owls have a higher overall level of activation.
    b. owls and larks are subjective categories and cannot be distinguished by biological patterns.
    c. owls have a peak in body temperature earlier than do larks.
    d. larks have higher body temperatures in the morning but lower temperatures in the evening than do owls.

14. According to the text, most North Americans get:
    a. too little sleep.
    b. just the right amount of sleep.
    c. too much sleep.
    d. too little sleep in childhood and too much as adults.

15. Psychologists believe that REM sleep serves a role in all of the following EXCEPT:
    a. learning complex skills.
    b. growing new neurons.
    c. erasing trivial memories.
    d. forming permanent memories.

16. Which of the following is a sleep disturbance during which a child partially awakens from Stage 4 sleep with a scream, is dazed, and in a panic state?
    a. sleep apnea
    b. somnambulism
    c. night terror
    d. narcolepsy

17. People who fall asleep suddenly at inappropriate times may have a sleep disorder called:
    a. narcolepsy.
    b. sleep apnea.
    c. social rudeness.
    d. somnambulism.

18. Which sleep disorder involves loud snoring and the cessation (stopping) of breathing during sleep?
    a. sleep apnea
    b. insomnia
    c. narcolepsy
    d. enuresis

19. Taking sleeping pills or a few drinks before bedtime usually results in all of the following EXCEPT:
    a. lighter sleep.
    b. less sleep overall.
    c. delayed sleep onset.
    d. more awakenings during the night.

20. Which of the following is a form of contemplation used to increase relaxation, block out worries and distractions, or foster a different form of consciousness?
    a. hypnosis
    b. cognitive withdrawal
    c. hypermnesia
    d. meditation

21. Hypnosis has proven most useful in treating:
    a. obesity.
    b. pain.
    c. drug abuse.
    d. alcoholism.

22. Which of the following is true regarding psychological dependence on drugs?
    a. It is easier to combat than physical addiction.
    b. It is harder to overcome than physical addiction.
    c. It is as difficult to overcome as physical addiction.
    d. There is no such thing.

23. Which part of our brain acts as our biological clock?
    a. circadian lobe
    b. thalamus
    c. pons
    d. suprachiasmatic nucleus

| Question Number | Answer | Learning Objective | Explanation for application questions |
| --- | --- | --- | --- |
| 1. | b. | 4.5 | |
| 2. | c. | 4.10 | |
| 3. | a. | 4.1 | Circadian rhythms fluctuate in regular patterns in a 24-hour period. |
| 4. | c. | 4.1 | |
| 5. | b. | 4.1 | |
| 6. | c. | 4.3 | |
| 7. | d. | 4.3 | |
| 8. | c. | 4.4 | |
| 9. | c. | 4.6 | |
| 10. | c. | 4.6 | |
| 11. | a. | 4.7 | |
| 12. | c. | 4.7 | |
| 13. | d. | 4.7 | |
| 14. | a. | 4.8 | |
| 15. | b. | 4.9 | |
| 16. | c. | 4.13 | |
| 17. | a. | 4.15 | |
| 18. | a. | 4.16 | |
| 19. | c. | 4.17 | |
| 20. | d. | 4.18 | |
| 21. | b. | 4.19 | |
| 22. | b. | 4.20 | |
| 23. | d. | 4.2 | |

#  lossary for Text Language Enhancement

Students identified the following words from the text as needing more explanation. This page can be cut out, folded in half, and used as a bookmark for this chapter.

| term | definition |
| --- | --- |
| ramifications | the result of somthing |
| advocacy | act of defending someone |
| adage | an old saying |
| imprecise | not accurate |
| fluctuation | increases and decreases |
| disrupted | interfered with |
| abruptly | suddenly, quickly |
| synchronized | occur at the same time |
| restorative | to bring back to the original condition |
| darting | moving quickly |
| erection | penis elongated |
| substantial | real; strong or solid |
| fumble | reach for in a clumsy way |
| snooze button | button to push on alarm that gives you 5 minutes more sleep |
| stupor | lack of alertness |
| larks | birds that like early morning hours |
| party pooper | person who is not fun at parties |
| contrary | opposite |
| lapses | gaps and problems |
| nodding | starting to sleep |
| rebound | increased amount to make up for loss |
| consolidation | combining together |
| bizarre | weird, odd |
| recurring | happening again and again |
| gasp | try to breathe hard |
| jet lag | sleep problems due to flying to a different time zone |
| trance-like | daze or daydream-like |
| misconceptions | not understand |
| violate | break |
| cope with | deal with |
| thrill | excitement |
| craving | desire |
| urge | wanting |
| jittery | body feels jumpy |
| virtuoso | person with great skill or talent |
| mild jolt | small stimulation |
| apathy | lack of interest |
| slurred | unclear |

| term | definition |
|------|------------|
| staggering<br>drowsy<br>mimic | walking unevenly (drunk)<br>very sleepy<br>imitate |

## Thinking Critically

### Evaluation

The famous sleep researcher Wilse Webb wrote a book called Sleep, the Gentle Tyrant. From what you have learned about sleep, explain why this is or is not a fitting title.

### Point/Counterpoint

You hear much debate about the pros and cons of legalizing drugs. Present the most convincing argument possible to support each of these positions:

a. Illicit drugs should be legalized.

b. Illicit drugs should not be legalized.

### Psychology in Your Life

You have been asked to make a presentation to Grade 7 and 8 students about the dangers of drugs. What are the most persuasive general arguments you can give to convince them not to get involved with drugs? What are some convincing, specific arguments against using each of these drugs: alcohol, marijuana, cigarettes, and cocaine?

| | |
|---|---|
| consciousness | slow-wave sleep |
| altered state of consciousness | delta wave |
| circadian rhythm | Stage 4 sleep |
| subjective night | microsleep |
| NREM sleep | REM rebound |
| REM sleep | REM dreams |
| sleep cycle | NREM dreams |

| | |
|---|---|
| Stage 3 and Stage 4 sleep; deep sleep. | The continuous stream of perceptions, thoughts, feelings, or sensations that we are aware of from moment to moment. |
| The slowest brain-wave pattern, associated with Stage 3 sleep and Stage 4 sleep. | A mental state other than ordinary waking consciousness, such as sleep, meditation, hypnosis, or a drug-induced state. |
| The deepest NREM stage of sleep, characterized by an EEG pattern of more than 50 percent delta waves. | Within each 24-hour period, the regular fluctuation from high to low points of certain bodily functions. |
| A momentary lapse from wakefulness into sleep, usually occurring when one has been sleep deprived. | The time during a 24-hour period when your body temperature is lowest and when your biological clock is telling you to go to sleep. |
| The increased amount of REM sleep that occurs after REM deprivation; often associated with unpleasant dreams or nightmares. | Non-rapid eye movement sleep, consisting of the four sleep stages and characterized by slow, regular respiration and heart rate, and absence of rapid eye movements. |
| A type of dream having a dreamlike and storylike quality and occurring almost continuously during each REM period; more vivid, visual, and emotional than NREM dreams. | Sleep characterized by rapid eye movements, paralysis of large muscles, fast and irregular heart rate and respiration rate, increased brain-wave activity, and vivid dreams. |
| Mental activity occurring during NREM sleep that is more thought-like in quality than REM dreams are. | A cycle of sleep lasting about 90 minutes and including one or more stages of NREM sleep followed by a period of REM sleep. |

| | |
|---|---|
| lucid dream | meditation |
| somnambulism | hypnosis |
| sleep terror | psychoactive drug |
| nightmare | minor tranquillizers |
| narcolepsy | physical drug dependence |
| sleep apnea | drug tolerance |
| insomnia | withdrawal symptoms |

| | |
|---|---|
| A group of techniques that involve focusing attention on an object, a word, one's breathing, or body movement in order to block out all distractions and achieve an altered state of consciousness. | A dream during which the dreamer is aware of dreaming and is often able to influence the content of the dream while it is in progress. |
| A trancelike state of concentrated, focused attention, heightened suggestibility, and diminished response to external stimuli. | Sleepwalking that occurs during a partial arousal from Stage 4 sleep. |
| A drug that alters normal mental functioning—mood, perception, or thought; if used medically, called a controlled substance. | A sleep disturbance in which a person partially awakens from Stage 4 sleep with a scream, dazed and groggy, in a panicked state, and with a racing heart. |
| A central nervous system depressant that calms the user (examples: Valium, Librium, Dalmane, Xanax). | A very frightening dream occurring during REM sleep. |
| A compulsive pattern of drug use in which the user develops a drug tolerance coupled with unpleasant withdrawal symptoms when the drug is discontinued. | A serious sleep disorder characterized by excessive daytime sleepiness and sudden, uncontrollable attacks of REM sleep. |
| A condition in which the user becomes progressively less affected by the drug so that larger and larger doses are necessary to maintain the same effect. | A sleep disorder characterized by periods when breathing stops during sleep and the person must awaken briefly in order to breathe; major symptoms are excessive daytime sleepiness and loud snoring. |
| The physical and psychological symptoms (usually opposite of those produced by the drug) that occur when the drug is discontinued. | A sleep disorder characterized by difficulty falling or staying asleep or by light, restless, or poor sleep, and causing distress and impaired daytime functioning. |

| | |
|---|---|
| psychological drug dependence | LSD |
| stimulants | flashback |
| amphetamines | marijuana and THC |
| cocaine and crack | heroin |
| crash | depressants |
| narcotics | alcohol |
| hallucinogens | barbiturates |

| | |
|---|---|
| A powerful hallucinogen with unpredictable effects ranging from perceptual changes and vivid hallucinations to states of panic and terror. | A craving or irresistible urge for a drug's pleasurable effects. |
| The brief recurrence, occurring suddenly and without warning at a later time, of effects a person has experienced while taking LSD. | A category of drugs that speed up activity in the central nervous system, suppress appetite, and cause a person to feel more awake, alert, and energetic; also called "uppers." |
| A hallucinogen with effects ranging from relaxation and giddiness to perceptual distortions and hallucinations. The second term is the principal psychoactive ingredient in marijuana and hashish. | A class of CNS stimulants that increase arousal, relieve fatigue, and suppress the appetite. |
| A highly addictive, partly synthetic narcotic derived from morphine. | A type of stimulant that produces a feeling of euphoria. The second term is the most potent, inexpensive, and addictive form of cocaine, and the form that is smoked. |
| A category of drugs that decrease activity in the central nervous system, slow down bodily functions, and reduce sensitivity to outside stimulation; also called "downers." | The feelings of depression, exhaustion, irritability, and anxiety that occur following an amphetamine or cocaine high. |
| A central nervous system depressant. | A class of depressant drugs that are derived from the opium poppy, and have pain-relieving and calming effects. |
| A central nervous system depressant that calms the user (examples: Valium, Librium, Xanax). | A category of drugs, sometimes called psychedelic, that alter perceptions and mood and can cause hallucinations. |

| | |
|---|---|
| suprachiasmatic nucleus | parasomnias |
| hallucination | ecstasy (MDMA) |
| downers | uppers |
| | |
| | |
| | |

| Sleep disturbances in which behaviours and physiological states that normally occur only in the waking state take place during sleep or in the transition from sleep to wakefulness. | A tiny structure in the brain's hypothalamus that controls the timing of circadian rhythms; the biological clock. |
|---|---|
| A designer drug that is a hallucinogen-amphetamine, and can produce permanent damage of the serotonin-releasing neurons. | An imaginary sensation. |
| A slang term for stimulants. | A slang term for depressants. |
| | |
| | |
| | |

# LEARNING

This outline provides a way to organize your notes from both the text and the lecture. It will also serve as a review for the exam.

| Module 5.1 Classical Conditioning | 1. Pavlov and Classical Conditioning |
| --- | --- |
| | 2. The Elements and Processes in Classical Conditioning |
| |    a. The Reflex: We Can't Help It |
| |    b. The Conditioned and Unconditioned Stimulus and Response |
| |    c. Extinction and Spontaneous Recovery (see figure next page) |

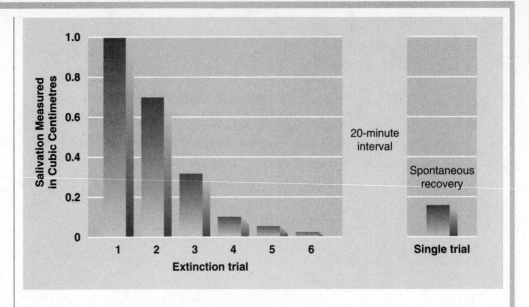

| Module 5.2 Operant Conditioning | 1. Skinner and Operant Conditioning |
|---|---|
| |    a. Shaping Behaviour |
| |    b. Superstitious Behaviour |
| |    c. Extinction |
| |    d. Generalization and Discrimination |
| | 2. Reinforcement: What's the Payoff? |
| |    a. Positive and Negative Reinforcement |
| |    b. Primary and Secondary Reinforcers |
| |    c. Schedules of Reinforcement |
| |       • Fixed-Ratio Schedule |
| |       • Variable-Ratio Schedule |
| |       • Fixed-Interval Schedule |
| |       • Variable-Interval Schedule |
| |    d. The Effect of Continuous and Partial Reinforcement on Extinction |
| | 3. Factors Influencing Operant Conditioning |

| | 4. Punishment: Less Is Best! |
|---|---|
| | 5. Escape and Avoidance Learning |
| | 6. Learned Helplessness |
| Module 5.3 Comparing Classical and Operant Conditioning | 1. What is the Difference? |
| Module 5.4 Behaviour Modification: Changing Our Act | 1. What is Behaviour Modification? |
| | 2. What Are Token Ecoomies? |
| Module 5.5 Cognitive Learning | 1. Observational Learning: Watching and Learning |
| |    a. Learning Aggression |
| Apply It! | • Overcoming Procrastination |

# Chapter Learning Objective Questions

Answer the following questions in the space provided and check your answers on the page numbers listed.

5.1 What was Pavlov's major contribution to psychology? p. 141

5.2 How is classical conditioning accomplished? p. 142

5.3 How does extinction occur in classical conditioning? p. 142

5.4 What is generalization? p. 144

5.5 What is discrimination in classical conditioning? p. 144

5.6 How did John Watson demonstrate that fear could be classically conditioned? p. 145

5.7 What are four factors that influence classical conditioning? p. 146

5.8 What types of responses can be learned through classical conditioning? p. 148

5.9 How are responses acquired through operant conditioning? p. 151

5.10 How is shaping used to condition a response? p. 151

5.11 How does extinction occur in operant conditioning? p. 152

5.12 What are the goals of both positive and negative reinforcement, and how are the goals accomplished for each? p. 153

5.13 What are the four major schedules of reinforcement, and which schedule yields the highest response rate and the greatest resistance to extinction? p. 154

5.14 What is the partial-reinforcement effect? p. 156

5.15 What three factors, in addition to the schedule of reinforcement, influence operant conditioning? p. 157

5.16 How does punishment differ from negative reinforcement? p. 157

5.17 What are some disadvantages of punishment? p. 158

5.18 What three factors increase the effectiveness of punishment? p. 159

5.19 What processes are comparable in classical and operant conditioning? p. 161

5.20 What is behaviour modification? p. 162

5.21 What is observational learning? p. 163

# Study Tips          Try It

Learn to study more effectively and improve your memory with these tips and practical exercises.

## Tips on Test Taking

### Multiple-choice questions

1. Check the directions to see if the questions call for more than one answer.
2. Answer each question in your head before you look at the possible answers; otherwise you may be confused by the choices.
3. Mark questions you can't answer immediately and come back to them if you have time.
4. If incorrect answers are not deducted from your score, use the following guidelines to guess:
   - If two answers are similar, except for one or two words, choose one of these answers.
   - If two answers have similar sounding or looking words, choose one of these answers.
   - If the answer calls for a sentence completion, eliminate the answers that would not form grammatically correct sentences.
   - If answers cover a numerical range, choose one in the middle.
   - If all else fails, close your eyes and pick one.

### True-False Questions

1. Answer these questions quickly.
2. Don't invest a lot of time unless they are worth many points.
3. If any part of the true-false statement is false, the whole statement is false.
4. Absolute qualifiers such as "always" or "never" generally indicate a false statement.

### Machine-Graded Tests

1. Check the test against the answer sheet often.
2. Watch for stray marks that look like answers.

### Open-Book and Notes Tests

1. Write down key points on a separate sheet.
2. Tape flags onto important pages of the book.
3. Number your notes and write a table of contents.
4. Prepare thoroughly because they are usually the most difficult tests.

### Essay Questions

1. Find out precisely what the question is asking. Don't *explain* when asked to *compare*.
2. Make an outline before writing. (Mindmaps work well, see Study Tips Chapter 6.)
3. Be brief, write clearly, use a pen, get to the point, and use examples.

## Behavioural Self-Management

1. Choose a target behaviour. Identify the activity you want to change.
2. Record a baseline. Count the number of desired or undesired responses you make each day.
3. Establish goals. Remember the principle of shaping and set realistic goals for gradual improvement in each successive week. Set daily goals that add up to the weekly goal.
4. Choose reinforcers. Set up daily rewards and weekly rewards that are meaningful to you.
5. Record your progress.
6. Collect and enjoy your rewards.
7. Adjust your plan as needed.

### Behavioural Contract

If you have trouble sticking with the above steps, try a behavioural contract. In the contract you state a specific problem behaviour you want to control, or a goal you want to achieve. Also state the rewards you will receive, privileges you will forfeit, or punishments you must accept. The contract should be typed and signed by you and a person you trust.

### Good Ways to Break Bad Habits

Extinction

Try to discover what is reinforcing a response and remove, avoid, or delay the reinforcement.

Alternate Responses

Try to get the same reinforcement with new responses. For example, if you want to stop smoking but you realize your smoking provides you with your only breaks at work, try taking a walk in the fresh air whenever you want a cigarette.

Cues

Avoid the cues that precede the bad habit you are trying to break. For example, don't walk in the supermarket door by the bakery if you are trying not to eat sweets.

Incompatible Responses

Do something that is incompatible with your bad habit. For example, if you do a jigsaw puzzle while you watch T.V. you can't eat.

# What Causes Forgetting?

This is a pertinent question for psychology students given that you are learning new material and you want to be able to remember what you have learned. It could help if you first know what contributes to your forgetting. Two of the main causes of forgetting are:

1. **Encoding Failure**—You don't even encode the information into long-term memory in the first place. This may occur if you assume a passive role in preparing for tests (e.g., merely reading and rereading your text). To avoid encoding failure, test yourself on the material frequently.

2. **Interference**—New information or information you have already learned interferes with the material you are trying to recall. To lessen the effects of interference on memory:

   a. When possible, study before going to sleep.

   b. Review material before going to sleep.

   c. Try not to study subjects back-to-back. Take short breaks between study sessions.

   d. Schedule your classes so that you do not attend courses with similar content back-to-back.

After studying the text and completing the Study Guide activities, answer these questions to determine if you need to review any areas before your exam.

1. Learning is any relatively permanent change in behaviour, capability, or attitude that is acquired through:
   a. cognition.
   b. experience.
   c. internal factors.
   d. maturation.

2. Ivan Pavlov, a Nobel Prize-winning physiologist, studied which of the following phenomena?
   a. maturation
   b. animal cognition
   c. operant conditioning
   d. classical conditioning

3. Which of the following is an example of an unconditioned reflex?
   a. Yvette's calling her mother every Sunday afternoon
   b. Josh's startled reaction when a car back-fires
   c. Carole's planting a vegetable garden every May
   d. Heather's turning up the radio whenever a Bruce Springsteen song is being played

4. In Pavlov's original research, dogs heard a tone and then had meat powder placed in their mouths, which caused them to salivate. After many pairings of the tone and the meat powder, they would salivate when the tone was presented alone. In this case, the salivating to the tone is an example of:
   a. a conditioned stimulus.
   b. an unconditioned stimulus.
   c. a conditioned response.
   d. an unconditioned response.

5. Which of the following elements in classical conditioning are learned?
   a. US and UR
   b. US and CR
   c. CS and UR
   d. CS and CR

6. Little Tammy is frightened by thunder and cries when she hears it. During a season of frequent electrical storms, thunder is always preceded by lightning. Now Tammy cries as soon as she sees lightning. In this example, the conditioned response is:
   a. thunder.
   b. lightning.
   c. crying at the sound of thunder.
   d. crying at the sight of lightning.

7. A puff of air on the surface of your eye will make you blink reflexively. If you hear a buzzer repeatedly just before air is puffed into your eye, eventually you will blink as soon as you hear the buzzer. In this example, the unconditioned stimulus is the:
   a. eyeblink response to the buzzer.
   b. buzzer.
   c. puff of air.
   d. eyeblink response to the puff of air.

8. When a conditioned stimulus is repeatedly presented without the unconditioned stimulus:
   a. extinction occurs.
   b. stimulus generalization occurs.
   c. higher-order conditioning occurs.
   d. remission occurs.

9. What key factor led Pavlov to determine that an extinguished conditioned response was not erased or forgotten, but only inhibited?
   a. The conditioned stimulus still appears to create an orienting reflex.
   b. The conditioned response could be recovered in less time than was originally required to learn it.
   c. Brain scans indicated that a permanent change at the synapses had occurred.
   d. The neutral stimulus was no longer neutral.

10. Scott developed a fear of dogs after having been bitten by a collie. The fact that Scott is now fearful of all dogs suggests:
    a. discrimination.
    b. extinction.
    c. spontaneous recovery.
    d. generalization.

11. What is the term for the learned ability to distinguish between similar stimuli so that the conditioned response occurs only to the original conditioned stimulus but not to the similar stimuli?
    a. generalization
    b. discrimination
    c. extinction
    d. spontaneous recovery

12. Advertisers place beautiful people or likeable places and objects with the products they are trying to sell because these items:
    a. distract from the disadvantages of the product.
    b. cause pleasant feelings to be evoked.
    c. are part of the product's basic qualities.
    d. are just elements of scenery.

13. An intense dislike of a particular food associated with nausea or discomfort is known as:
    a. an avoidance learning.
    b. a taste aversion.
    c. higher-order conditioning.
    d. spontaneous recovery.

14. Operant conditioning has been researched most extensively by:
    a. John B. Watson.
    b. Edward Thorndike.
    c. B. F. Skinner.
    d. Ivan Pavlov.

15. In the psychology of learning, any event or object that strengthens or increases the probability of the response it follows is known as:
    a. the law of effect.
    b. a reinforcer.
    c. a punishment.
    d. an aversive stimulus.

16. According to operant conditioning, behaviours change because of the:
    a. involuntary associations formed between stimulus and response.
    b. consequences they produced.
    c. unconscious motivations involved.
    d. observation of other people's behaviours.

17. The technique that teaches complex behaviours by first reinforcing small steps toward the behavioural goal is called:
    a. training.
    b. approximating.
    c. molding.
    d. shaping.

18. What can occur if a person believes that a connection exists between an act and its consequences when there is no relationship between the two?
    a. classical conditioning
    b. superstitious behaviour
    c. shaping
    d. sequential learning

19. According to the principles of operant conditioning, what would be the best way to extinguish temper tantrums in a child?
    a. Punish the child after each temper tantrum.
    b. Punish some of the temper tantrums and ignore the rest.
    c. Never ever give the child what he or she wants during a temper tantrum.
    d. After the tantrum is over, give the child what he or she wanted as a reward for ending the tantrum.

20. An event that increases the probability of a response by removing an unpleasant stimulus is called:
    a. positive reinforcement.
    b. negative reinforcement.
    c. primary reinforcement.
    d. secondary reinforcement.

21. The gold star the teacher gives Tyrone for spelling all the words correctly is a:
    a. contingent reward.
    b. primary reinforcer.
    c. discriminative stimulus.
    d. secondary reinforcer.

| Question Number | Answer | Learning Objective | Explanation for application questions |
|---|---|---|---|
| 1. | b. | 5.1 | |
| 2. | d. | 5.1 | |
| 3. | b. | 5.1 | We are born with reacting to loud noises, which means the car backfiring is an unconditioned stimulus. |
| 4. | c. | 5.2 | |
| 5. | d. | 5.2 | |
| 6. | d. | 5.2 | Tammy had to learn to be afraid of the lightning because it was associated with a loud noise. Conditioned responses are learned. |
| 7. | c. | 5.2 | |
| 8. | a. | 5.3 | |
| 9. | b. | 5.3 | |
| 10. | d. | 5.4 | Generalization occurs when we generalize our reaction to similar stimuli. |
| 11. | b. | 5.4 | |
| 12. | b. | 5.8 | |
| 13. | b. | 5.7 | |
| 14. | c. | 5.9 | |
| 15. | b. | 5.9 | |
| 16. | b. | 5.10 | |
| 17. | d. | 5.11 | |
| 18. | b. | 5.11 | Superstitious behaviour occurs when we believe two things are related even when they are not. |
| 19. | c. | 5.13 | |
| 20. | b. | 5.14 | |
| 21. | d. | 5.14 | Primary reinforcers are rewards that directly meet needs, such as food and water. Secondary reinforcers enable us to meet needs indirectly. |

# Glossary for Text Language Enhancement

Students identified the following words from the text as needing more explanation. This page can be cut out, folded in half, and used as a bookmark for this chapter.

| term | definition |
|---|---|
| vicious | mean |
| extortion | using threat of force to take money from someone |
| reign of terror | a time during which many people are hurt |
| maturation | process of becoming fully grown |
| exclude | reject |
| infer | deduce from evidence |
| incision | cut |
| different avenues | various ways |
| meticulous | very exact and careful |
| hermetically | perfectly airtight |
| girders | beams |
| embedded | buried |
| moat | trench around building |
| vibrations | back and forward movement |
| adjoining | connected |
| puff of air | quick and forceful movement of air |
| buzzers | make "zzzzz" sounds |
| striking | hitting |
| acquisition | to gain or acquire |
| formulated | created |
| phenomenon | a notable thing |
| sanction | approve |
| drug-craving | very powerfully desiring drugs |
| drug paraphernalia | things used to take drugs |
| steel | a very strong metal |
| elicit | make happen |
| optimal | best |
| aversion | wanting to avoid |
| emitted | gave off or performed |
| food pellets | small hard food pieces |
| disruptive | disturbing |
| amazing feats | impressive acts |
| temper tantrum | act out violently |
| erratic | not the usual or expected |
| disks | circles |
| peck | hit with beak |
| unwittingly | without knowing |
| nagging | constant complaining |
| magnitude | size |

| term | definition |
|---|---|
| in conjunction with | along with |
| discharging anger | getting rid of anger |
| token | something that has an agreed-upon worth, for exchange |
| consciousness raising | making people aware of something |
| pervasiveness | being everywhere |
| Bobo Doll | inflatable punching bag |

# Thinking Critically

## Evaluation

Prepare statements outlining the strengths and limitations of classical conditioning, operant conditioning, and observational learning in explaining how behaviours are acquired and maintained.

## Point/Counterpoint

The use of behaviour modification has been a source of controversy among psychologists and others. Prepare arguments supporting each of the following positions:

a.  Behaviour modification should be used in society to shape the behaviour of others.

b.  Behaviour modification should not be used in society to shape the behaviour of others.

## Psychology in Your Life

Think of a behaviour of a friend, a family member, or a professor that you would like to change. Using what you know about classical conditioning, operant conditioning, and observational learning, formulate a detailed plan for changing the behaviour of the target person.

| | |
|---|---|
| stimulus | conditioned stimulus (CS) |
| learning | conditioned response (CR) |
| classical conditioning | extinction (in classical conditioning) |
| reflex | spontaneous recovery |
| conditioned reflex | generalization |
| unconditioned response (UR) | discrimination |
| unconditioned stimulus (US) | higher-order conditioning |

| | |
|---|---|
| A neutral stimulus that, after repeated pairing with an unconditioned stimulus, becomes associated with it and elicits a conditioned response. | Any event or object in the environment to which an organism responds; plural is *stimuli*. |
| That response that comes to be elicited by a conditioned stimulus as a result of its repeated pairing with an unconditioned stimulus. | A relatively permanent change in behaviour, capability, or attitude that is acquired through experience and cannot be attributed to illness, injury, or maturation. |
| The weakening and often eventual disappearance of a learned response (in classical conditioning, the repeated presentation of the conditioned stimulus without the unconditioned stimulus). | A process through which a response previously made only to a specific stimulus is made to another stimulus that has been paired repeatedly with the original stimulus. |
| The reappearance of an extinguished response when an organism is exposed to the original conditioned stimulus following a rest period. | An involuntary response to a particular stimulus, like the eyeblink response to a puff of air or salivation to food placed in the mouth. |
| In classical conditioning, making a response to a stimulus similar to the original conditioned stimulus; in operant conditioning, making the learned response to a stimulus similar to the one for which it was originally reinforced. | A learned reflex rather than a naturally occurring one. |
| The learned ability to distinguish between similar stimuli so that the conditioned response occurs only to the original conditioned stimulus but not to similar stimuli. | A response that is invariably elicited by the unconditioned stimulus without prior learning. |
| Occurs when a neutral stimulus is paired with an existing conditioned stimulus, becomes associated with it, and gains the power to elicit the same conditioned response. | A stimulus that elicits a specific response without prior learning. |

| | |
|---|---|
| drug tolerance | shaping |
| taste aversion | successive approximations |
| | extinction (in operant conditioning) |
| | discriminative stimulus |
| operant conditioning | reinforcement |
| reinforcer | positive reinforcement |
| Skinner box | negative reinforcement |

| | |
|---|---|
| Gradually modifying a desired behaviour by reinforcing responses that become progressively closer to it; reinforcing successive approximates of the desired response. | A condition in which the user becomes progressively less affected by a drug so that larger and larger doses are necessary to maintain the same effect. |
| A series of gradual training steps, with each step becoming more like the final desired response. | The dislike and/or avoidance of a particular food that has been associated with nausea or discomfort. |
| The weakening and often eventual disappearance of a learned response (in operant conditioning, the conditioned response is weakened by withholding reinforcement). | |
| A stimulus that signals whether a certain response or behaviour is likely to be followed by reward or punishment. | |
| An event that follows a response and increases the strength of the response and/or the likelihood that it will be repeated. | A type of learning in which the consequences of behaviour tend to increase or decrease that behaviour in the future. |
| A reward or pleasant consequence that follows a response and increases the probability that the response will be repeated. | Anything that strengthens a response or increases the probability that it will occur. |
| The termination of an unpleasant stimulus after a response in order to increase the probability that the response will be repeated. | A soundproof operant conditioning changer with a device for delivering food and either a bar for rats to press or a disk for pigeons to peck. |

| | |
|---|---|
| primary reinforcer | fixed-interval schedule |
| secondary reinforcer | variable-interval schedule |
| continuous reinforcement | partial-reinforce-ment effect |
| partial reinforcement | punishment |
| schedule of reinforcement | avoidance learning |
| fixed-ratio schedule | learned helplessness |
| variable-ratio schedule | |

| | |
|---|---|
| A schedule in which a reinforcer is given following the first correct response after a fixed period of time has elapsed. | A reinforcer that fulfills a basic physical need for survival and does not depend on learning. |
| A schedule in which the reinforcer is given after the first correct response following a varying time of non-reinforcement based on an average time. | A neutral stimulus that becomes reinforcing after repeated pairings with other reinforcers. |
| The greater resistance to extinction that occurs when a portion, rather than all, of the correct responses are reinforced. | Reinforcement that is administered after every desired or correct response; the most effective method of conditioning a new response. |
| The removal of a pleasant stimulus or the application of an unpleasant stimulus, which tends to suppress a response. | A pattern of reinforcement in which some portion, rather than 100 percent, of the correct responses are reinforced. |
| Learning to avoid events or conditions associated with dreaded or aversive outcomes. | A systematic program for administering reinforcements that has a predictable effect on behaviour. |
| The learned response of resigning oneself passively to aversive conditions, rather than taking action to change them; learned through repeated exposure to unavoidable aversive events. | A schedule in which a reinforcer is given after a fixed number of correct responses. |
| | A schedule in which a reinforcer is given after a varying number of non-reinforced responses based on an average ratio. |

| behaviour modification | cognitive processes |
|---|---|
| token economy | |
| observational learning | |
| modelling | |
| model | |
| | |
| | |

| | |
|---|---|
| Mental processes such as thinking, knowing, problem-solving, and remembering. | Systematic application of the learning principles of operant conditioning, classical conditioning, or observational learning to individuals or groups in order to eliminate undesirable behaviour or encourage desirable behaviour. |
| | A program that motivates and reinforces socially acceptable behaviours with tokens that can be exchanged for desired items or privileges. |
| | Learning by observing the behaviour of others and the consequences of that behaviour; learning by imitation. |
| | Another name for observational learning. |
| | The individual who demonstrates a behaviour or serves as an example in observational learning. |
| | |
| | |

# 6

# MEMORY

**Module 6.1 Remembering**

## 1. The Three Processes in Memory

**The Processes Required in Remembering**

**Encoding**
Transforming information into a form that can be stored in memory

→

**Storage**
Maintaining information in memory

→

**Retrieval**
Bringing stored material to mind

## 2. The Three Memory Systems

**The Three Memory Systems**

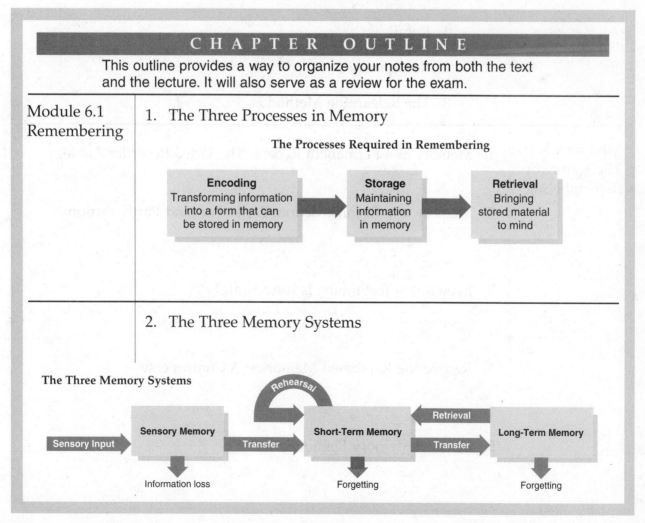

Sensory Input → **Sensory Memory** → Transfer → **Short-Term Memory** ⇄ Retrieval / Transfer ⇄ **Long-Term Memory**

Rehearsal

Information loss — Forgetting — Forgetting

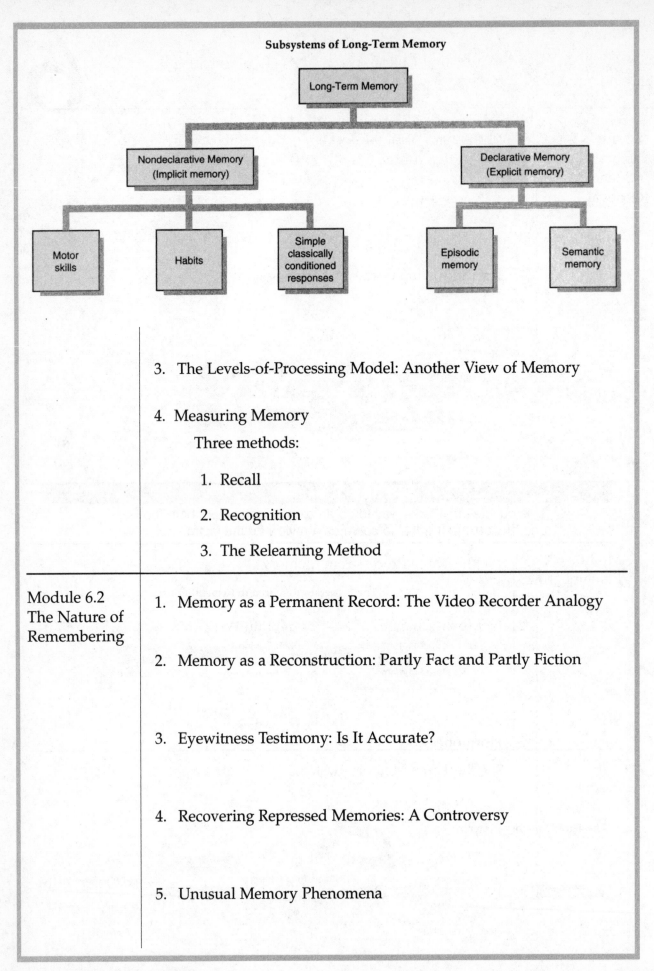

**Subsystems of Long-Term Memory**

Long-Term Memory

Nondeclarative Memory (Implicit memory)

Declarative Memory (Explicit memory)

Motor skills

Habits

Simple classically conditioned responses

Episodic memory

Semantic memory

3. The Levels-of-Processing Model: Another View of Memory

4. Measuring Memory

   Three methods:

   1. Recall

   2. Recognition

   3. The Relearning Method

**Module 6.2 The Nature of Remembering**

1. Memory as a Permanent Record: The Video Recorder Analogy

2. Memory as a Reconstruction: Partly Fact and Partly Fiction

3. Eyewitness Testimony: Is It Accurate?

4. Recovering Repressed Memories: A Controversy

5. Unusual Memory Phenomena

| | |
|---|---|
| World of Psychology | • Memory and Culture |
| Module 6.3 Factors Influencing Retrieval | 1. The Serial Position Effect: To Be Remembered, Be First or Last but Not in the Middle<br><br>2. Environmental Context and Memory<br><br>3. The State-Dependent Memory Effect |
| Module 6.4 Biology and Memory | 1. Brain Damage: A Clue to Memory Formation<br><br>2. Neuronal Changes in Memory:  Brain Work<br><br>3. Hormones and Memory |

| Module 6.5 Forgetting | 1. Hermann Ebbinghaus and the First Experimental Studies on Learning and Memory |

**Ebbinghaus's Curve of Forgetting**

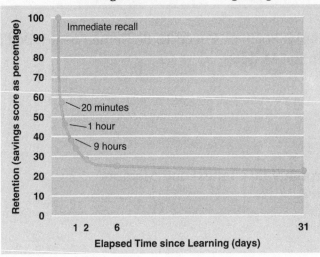

2. The Causes of Forgetting

   a. Encoding Failure

   b. Decay

   c. Interference

**Retroactive and Proactive Interference**

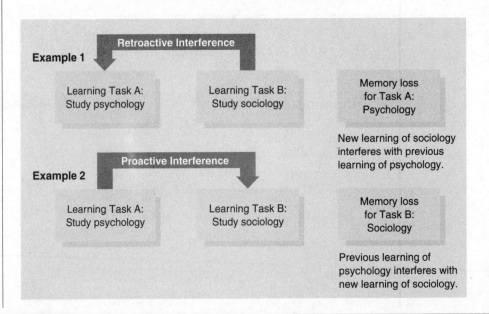

| | |
|---|---|
| | d. Consolidation Failure |
| | e. Motivated Forgetting: Don't Remind Me |
| | f. Retrieval Failure: Misplaced Memories |
| | g. Prospective Forgetting: Forgetting to Remember |
| Module 6.6 Improving Memory | 1. Study Habits That Aid Memory |
| Apply It! | • Improving Memory with Mnemonic Devices |

Answer the following questions in the space provided and check your answers on the page numbers listed.

6.1 What three processes are involved in the act of remembering? p. 174

6.2 What is sensory memory? p. 175–176

6.3 What are the characteristics of short-term memory? p. 177

6.4 What is long-term memory, and what are its subsystems? p. 179–180

6.5 What are three methods of measuring retention? p. 181

6.6 What is meant by the statement "Memory is reconstructive in nature"? p. 183

6.7 What is Bartlett's contribution to our understanding of memory? p. 183

6.8 What are schemas and how do they affect memory? p. 183

6.9 What conditions reduce the reliability of eyewitness testimony? p. 184

6.10 Does hypnosis improve the memory of eyewitnesses? p. 186

6.11 What is the serial position effect? p. 189

6.12 How does environmental context affect memory? p. 189

6.13 What is the state-dependent memory effect? p. 190

6.14 What has the study of H.M. revealed about the role of the hippocampus in memory? p. 191

6.15 What is long-term potentiation and why is it important? p. 193

6.16 How do memories of threatening situations compare with ordinary memories? p. 193

6.17 What was Ebbinghaus's major contribution to psychology? p. 194

6.18 What are six causes of forgetting? p. 195

6.19 What is interference, and how can it be minimized? p. 196

6.20 What are four study habits that can aid memory? p. 198

6.21 What is overlearning, and why is it important? p. 199

## Fill in the Information in the White Blocks

**The Processes Required in Remembering**

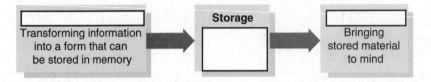

| | | |
|---|---|---|
| Transforming information into a form that can be stored in memory | Storage | Bringing stored material to mind |

**The Three Memory Systems**

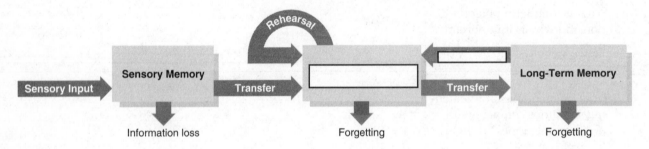

Sensory Input → Sensory Memory → Transfer → [ ] → Transfer → Long-Term Memory

Rehearsal

Information loss — Forgetting — Forgetting

**Subsystems of Long-Term Memory**

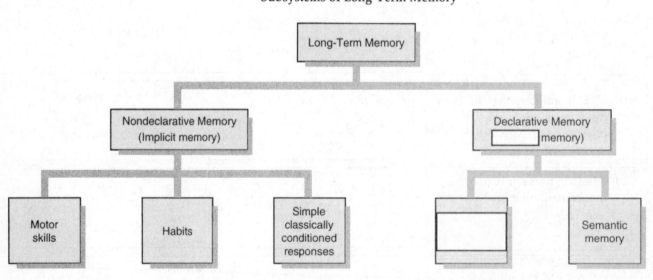

Long-Term Memory
- Nondeclarative Memory (Implicit memory)
  - Motor skills
  - Habits
  - Simple classically conditioned responses
- Declarative Memory ( ___ memory)
  - [ ]
  - Semantic memory

Learn to study more effectively and improve your memory with these tips and practical exercises.

## Reading for Remembering

1. **Skim**
   Skim the entire chapter.
2. **Outline**
   Read the outline at the front of the chapter in the text.
3. **Questions**
   Write out several questions that come to your mind that you think will be answered in the chapter.
4. **Read** the material.
5. **Highlight**
   While reading, highlight the most important information (no more than 10%).
6. **Answers**
   As you read get the answers to your questions.
7. **Recite**
   When you finish reading an assignment, make a speech about it.  Recite the key points.
8. **Review**
   Plan your first review within 24 hours.
9. **Review again**
   Weekly reviews are important—perhaps only four or five minutes per assignment. Go over your notes. Read the highlighted parts of your text. Recite the more complicated points.

### More about Review

You can do short reviews any time, anywhere, if you are prepared. Take your text to the dentist's office, and if you don't have time to read a whole assignment, review last week's assignment. Conduct five-minute reviews when you are waiting for water to boil. Three-by-five cards work well for review. Write ideas and facts on cards and carry them with you. These short review periods can be effortless and fun.

## Try Your Own Mnemonics

Chapter 6 in your textbook discusses mnemonics. Most memory experts agree that mnemonics are very powerful tools. Here are some additional pointers so you can make up your own mnemonics.

1. Turn information into mental pictures. We remember pictures better than words, and the funnier or more unusual the better.

2. Make things meaningful to you.

3. Connect the information to what you already know.

### Example

To remember how much information short-term and long-term memory can hold, picture a huge group of people standing on the grass in a park. The seven people standing closest to you have unusually short legs and all the rest of the people have unusually long legs. (Remember we said funny is good.) The short-legged people represent the fact that we are able to hold an average of 7 items in short-term memory. The many long-legged people represent that long-term memory is practically unlimited.

**Now think of one of your own and write it here.**

After studying the text and completing the Study Guide activities, answer these questions to determine if you need to review any areas before your exam.

1. To transform sensory input into a form that is more readily processed by one's memory is to _____ the input.
   a. retrieve
   b. chunk
   c. rehearse
   d. encode

2. The second stage of information processing for memory maintenance is:
   a. encoding.
   b. storage.
   c. retrieval.
   d. episodic.

3. The memory process of locating and returning stored information to the conscious state is referred to as:
   a. encoding.
   b. procedural encoding.
   c. storage.
   d. retrieval.

4. An usher points out a seat to Paul in a darkened theatre by moving a flashlight in a rectangular motion. Paul sees the form of the rectangle because images from the flashlight are being briefly stored in his:
   a. semantic memory.
   b. short-term memory.
   c. photographic memory.
   d. sensory memory.

5. Working memory is another term for:
   a. iconic memory.
   b. semantic memory.
   c. elaborative rehearsal.
   d. short-term memory.

6. In the _____ memory the stimulus tends to fade significantly after 20 to 30 seconds if it is not repeated.
   a. iconic and echoic
   b. sensory
   c. long-term
   d. short-term

7. Jamie meets someone at a party and wants to remember his name. To do this, she repeats his name over and over in her mind. This process is called:
   a. rehearsal.
   b. consolidation.
   c. categorization.
   d. indexing.

8. The memory of events experienced by a person is known as:
   a. procedural memory.
   b. semantic memory.
   c. iconic memory.
   d. episodic memory.

9. When another student tells you that he knows the three kinds of memory, he is using:
   a. semantic memory.
   b. episodic memory.
   c. procedural memory.
   d. metamemory.

10. Knowledge and memory of the steps involved in riding a bicycle are a result of _____ memory.
    a. echoic
    b. implicit
    c. semantic
    d. episodic

11. The short-term memory can hold _____ chunks of information at any one time.
    a. 3
    b. 7
    c. 10
    d. 12

12. The type(s) of memory capable of virtually permanent storage is the:
    a. long-term memory.
    b. short-term memory.
    c. sensory memory.
    d. iconic and echoic memories.

13. The easiest type of memory task is:
    a. recall.
    b. recognition.
    c. relearning.
    d. savings.

14. Multiple-choice tests such as this one measure _____ memory tasks.
    a. recall
    b. recognition
    c. relearning
    d. savings

15. The method of savings is used to investigate:
    a. recall.
    b. readiness.
    c. recognition.
    d. relearning.

16. According to Ebbinghaus's curve of forgetting, forgetting occurs most rapidly:
    a. approximately 31 days after learning.
    b. immediately after the material is learned.
    c. during the learning process.
    d. during stress.

17. In psychoanalytic theory, the ejection of anxiety-evoking ideas from our conscious awareness is called:
    a. elaborative rehearsal.
    b. displacement.
    c. repression.
    d. regression.

18. We may forget because of experiences that occur before or after learning something new according to the:
    a. decay theory.
    b. interference theory.
    c. motivation theory.
    d. engram theory.

19. Justin believes that we reconstruct our recollections by elaborating on pieces of information. Mike argues that our recollections are like accurate snapshots in our long-term memories. Carla states that we have faithful mental representation in our long-term memories.
    a. Justin is correct.
    b. Mike is correct.
    c. Carla is correct.
    d. All the above are correct.

20. Remembering in detail where you were and what you were doing when the news broke that the space shuttle *Challenger* had exploded would represent what memory experts call:
    a. flashbulb memory.
    b. episodic memory.
    c. state-dependent memory.
    d. eidetic memory.

21. If you visited your old high school building, you might recall events that occurred there much more easily. This type of memory stimulation is known as:
    a. environmental context.
    b. state-dependent memory.
    c. photographic memory.
    d. iconic memory.

22. When people feel anger, they may be reminded of other times of anger and frustration. This type of memory is known as:
    a. metamemory.
    b. working memory.
    c. context-dependent memory.
    d. state-dependent memory.

23. In the case of H. M., his operation prevented him from transferring information from his
    a. sensory memory to his short-term memory.
    b. short-term memory to his long-term memory.
    c. iconic memory to his acoustic memory.
    d. procedural memory to his semantic memory.

24. The _____ is a structure in the limbic system that plays an important role in the formation of new memories.
    a. thalamus
    b. Broca's area
    c. hippocampus
    d. parietal lobe

25. In a list of words, we would probably remember:
    a. the first and middle words.
    b. the first and last words.
    c. the middle and last words.
    d. just the middle words.

| Question Number | Answer | Learning Objective | Explanation for application questions |
|---|---|---|---|
| 1. | d. | 6.1 | |
| 2. | b. | 6.1 | |
| 3. | d. | 6.1 | Retrieval involves locating and retrieving stored information. |
| 4. | d. | 6.2 | Sensory memory holds onto sensations for a very brief period of time. |
| 5. | d. | 6.3 | Working memory and short-term memory are equivalent terms. |
| 6. | d. | 6.3 | Short-term memory only lasts a few seconds if we do not rehearse. |
| 7. | a. | 6.3 | Repeating something over and over is called rehearsal. |
| 8. | d. | 6.4 | Episodic memory refers to remembering the "episodes" of our lives. |
| 9. | a. | 6.4 | Semantic memory stores information like a dictionary. |
| 10. | b. | 6.4 | Implicit memory contains memories of skills we have learned. |
| 11. | b. | 6.3 | Short-term memory can hold about 7 items or chunks. |
| 12. | a. | 6.4 | Long-term memory can hold onto an unlimited amount of information virtually forever. |
| 13. | b. | 6.5 | It is easiest to recognize information. |
| 14. | b. | 6.5 | Multiple-choice questions mainly require recognition. |
| 15. | d. | 6.5 | |
| 16 | b. | 6.17 | Retention goes down dramatically after the first 9 hours. |
| 17. | c. | 6.18 | Elaborative rehearsal helps memory. |
| 18. | b. | 6.19 | |
| 19. | a. | 6.6 | |
| 20. | a. | 6.8 | |
| 21. | a. | 6.12 | The context is giving the retrieval cues. |
| 22. | d. | 6.9 | Internal physiology and emotions can serve as retrieval cues. This is called state-dependent learning. |
| 23. | b. | 6.10 | H. M. (case study in your textbook) could not transfer short-term memory into long-term memory. |
| 24. | c. | 6.10 | Hippocampus is important in the formation of new memories. |
| 25. | b. | 6.11 | We remember the first and last items on lists. |

# Glossary for Text Language Enhancement

Students identified the following words from the text as needing more explanation. This page can be cut out, folded in half, and used as a bookmark for this chapter.

| term | definition |
| --- | --- |
| stab | put a knife into |
| astonishing | surprising and shocking |
| alibi | the fact of being somewhere else when a crime was committed |
| rustling | moving about making noise |
| fades | becomes less easy to recall |
| disrupted | interfered with |
| floppy disk | disk for computer |
| analogy | similarity |
| discrete | separate |
| ingenious | good and useful |
| abundance | a large amount |
| acoustic form | by sound |
| chunks | larger pieces |
| rehearsal | repeating over and over |
| distraction | pulls attention away |
| semantic | meaning of something |
| repetitive | repeating |
| shallowest | opposite of deepest |
| retention | memory |
| cues | signs to help connection |
| to jog | help |
| seizure | convulsive fit |
| hinder | prevent |
| dashboard | panel of gauges in a car |
| haunt | keep coming to mind |
| flashbacks | strong memories |
| replica | copy |
| expectation | what a person thinks will happen |
| distort | change and bend |
| distortion | something that is changed |
| infallible | never wrong |
| hypnotized | in a trance-like state of consciousness |
| skeptical | uncertain something is truthful |
| vivid | strong and clear |
| constitute | make up |
| reinstated | brought back |
| intoxicated | drunk |
| sober | not drunk |

| term | definition |
|---|---|
| amphetamines | drugs that speed up |
| barbiturates | drugs that calm down |
| synapses | communication between nerve cells |
| haphazard | not organized |
| cramming | studying at last minute |

# Thinking Critically

## Evaluation

Some studies cited in this chapter involved only one or a few participants.

a. Select two of these studies and discuss the possible problems in drawing conclusions on the basis of studies using so few participants.

b. Suggest several possible explanations for the researchers' findings other than those proposed by the researchers.

c. In your view, should such studies even be mentioned in a textbook? Why or why not?

## Point/Counterpoint

Using what you have learned in this chapter on memory, prepare an argument citing cases and specific examples to support each of these positions:

a. Long-term memory is a permanent record of our experiences.

b. Long-term memory is not necessarily a permanent record of our experiences.

## Psychology in Your Life

Drawing upon your knowledge, formulate a plan that you can put into operation to help improve your memory and avoid the pitfalls that cause forgetting.

| | |
|---|---|
| encoding | rehearsal |
| storage | long-term memory |
| consolidation | nondeclarative memory |
| retrieval | declarative memory |
| sensory memory | episodic memory |
| short-term memory | semantic memory |
| displacement | levels-of-processing model |

| | |
|---|---|
| The act of purposely repeating information to maintain it in short-term memory or to transfer it to long-term memory. | Transforming information into a form that can be stored in short-term or long-term memory. |
| The relatively permanent memory system with a virtually unlimited capacity. | The act of maintaining information in memory. |
| The subsystem within long-term memory that consists of skills acquired through repetitive practice, habits, and simple classically conditioned responses; also called *implicit memory*. | The presumed process, believed to involve the hippocampus, by which a permanent memory is formed. |
| The subsystem within long-term memory that stores facts, information, and personal life experiences; also called *explicit memory*. | The act of bringing to mind material that has been stored in memory. |
| The subpart of declarative memory that contains memories of personally experienced events. | The memory system that holds information coming in through the senses for a period ranging from a fraction of a second to several seconds. |
| The subpart of declarative memory that stores general knowledge; our mental encyclopedia or dictionary. | The second state of memory, which holds about seven items for less than 30 seconds without rehearsal; working memory. |
| A single memory system model in which retention depends on how deeply information is processed. | The event that occurs when short-term memory is holding its maximum and each new item entering short-term memory pushes out an existing item. |

| | |
|---|---|
| recall | consolidation failure |
| retrieval cue | retrograde amnesia |
| recognition | decay theory |
| relearning method | interference |
| savings score | motivated forgetting |
| nonsense syllable | repression |
| encoding failure | amnesia |

| | |
|---|---|
| Any disruption in the consolidation process that prevents a permanent memory from forming. | A measure of retention that requires one to remember material with few or no retrieval cues, as in an essay test. |
| A loss of memory for events occurring for a period of time preceding a brain trauma that caused a loss of consciousness. | Any stimulus or bit of information that aids in the retrieval of particular information from long-term memory. |
| A theory of forgetting, which holds that the memory trace, if not used, disappears with the passage of time. | A measure of retention that requires one to identify material as familiar, or as having been encountered before. |
| Memory loss that occurs because information or associations stored either before or after a given memory hinder our ability to remember it. | Measuring retention in terms of the percentage of time or learning trials saved in relearning material compared with the time required to learn it originally; also called the savings method. |
| Forgetting through suppression or repression in order to protect oneself from material that is too painful, anxiety- or guilt-producing, or otherwise unpleasant. | The percentage of time or learning trials saved in relearning material over the amount of time or number of learning trials required for the original learning. |
| Removing from one's consciousness disturbing, guilt-provoking, or otherwise unpleasant memories so that one is no longer aware a painful event occurred. | A consonant-vowel-consonant combination that does not spell a word; used to control the meaningfulness of the material. |
| A partial or complete loss of memory resulting from brain trauma or psychological trauma. | A cause of forgetting resulting from material never having been put into long-term memory. |

| | |
|---|---|
| reconstruction | recency effect |
| schemas | state-dependent memory effect |
| selective attention | anterograde amnesia |
| flashbulb memory | |
| eidetic imagery | long-term potentiation |
| serial position effect | overlearning |
| primacy effect | massed practice |

| | |
|---|---|
| The tendency to recall the last items on a list more readily than those in the middle of the list. | A memory that is not an exact replica of an event but has been pieced together from a few highlights using information that may or may not be accurate. |
| The tendency to recall information better if one is in the same pharmacological or psychological state as when the information was encoded. | The integrated frameworks of knowledge and assumptions we have about people, objects, and events, which affect how we encode and recall information. |
| The inability to form long-term memories of events occurring after a brain injury or brain surgery, although memories formed before the trauma are usually intact. | Focusing on one piece of information while placing other information in the background. |
| | An extremely vivid memory of the conditions surrounding one's first hearing the news of a surprising, shocking, or highly emotional event. |
| A long-lasting increase in the efficiency of neural transmission at the synapses. | The ability to retain the image of a visual stimulus several minutes after it has been removed from view. |
| Practising or studying material beyond the point where it can be repeated once without error. | Upon presentation of a list of items, the tendency to remember the beginning and ending items better than the middle items. |
| One long learning practice session as opposed to spacing the learning in shorter practice sessions over an extended period. | The tendency to recall the first items on a list more readily than the middle items. |

# 7

# INTELLIGENCE, COGNITION, AND LANGUAGE

| Module 7.2 Measuring Intelligence | 1. Alfred Binet and the First Successful Intelligence Test |
| --- | --- |
| | 2. The Intelligence Quotient, or IQ |

$$\frac{\text{Mental Age}}{\text{Chronological Age}} \times 100 = \text{IQ}$$

3. Intelligence Testing in North America

   a. The Stanford-Binet Intelligence Scale

   b. Intelligence Testing for Adults

   c. The Wechsler Intelligence Tests

   d. Group Intelligence Tests

4. Requirements of Good Tests

   a. Reliability

   b. Validity

   c. Standardization

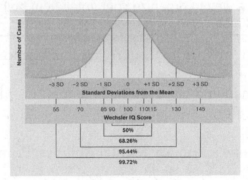

---

| Module 7.3 Measuring Intelligence | 1. Terman's Study of Gifted People |
| --- | --- |
| | 2. Who Is Gifted? |
| | 3. People with Mental Disabilities |

| | |
|---|---|
| Module 7.4 <br> The IQ <br> Controversy: <br> Brainy Dispute | 1. The Uses and Abuses of Intelligence Tests <br><br> a. Can IQ scores predict success and failure? <br><br> b. The abuses of intelligence tests: <br> Making too much of a single number <br><br><br> 2. The Nature–Nurture Controversy: Battle of the Centuries <br><br> **Correlations between the IQ Scores of Persons with Various Relationships** <br><br> <br><br> a. Behavioural Genetics: Investigating Nature and Nurture <br><br> b. A Natural Experiment: Identical Twins Reared Apart <br><br> 3. Intelligence: Is It Fixed or Changeable? <br><br> a. Race and IQ: The Controversial Views <br><br> • Is The Gap Due To Race Alone? |
| Module 7.5 <br> Emotional <br> Intelligence | 1. Personal Components of Emotional Intelligence <br><br> 2. Interpersonal Components of Emotional Intelligence |

| | |
|---|---|
| Module 7.8<br>Language | 1. The Structure of Language<br><br>    • Phonemes<br><br>    • Morphemes<br><br>    • Syntax<br><br>    • Semantics<br><br>2. Language Development<br><br>    • Cooing and Babbling<br><br>    • The One-Word Stage<br><br>    • The Two-Word Stage and Telegraphic Speech<br><br>    • Suffixes, Function Words, and Grammatical Rules<br><br>3. Theories of Language Development: How Do We Acquire It?<br><br>    • Learning Theory<br><br>    • The Nativist Position<br><br>    • The Interactionist Perspective<br><br>4. Having More Than One Language<br><br>5. Animal Language<br><br>6. Language and Thinking |
| Apply It! | • Building A Powerful Vocabulary<br><br>    1. Think Analytically<br><br>    2. Word Connections<br><br>    3. Knowledge of Word Parts |

Answer the following questions in the space provided and check your answers on the page numbers listed.

| | |
|---|---|
| 7.1 What factors underlie intelligence, according to Spearman, Thurstone, and Guilford? p. 208–209 | |
| 7.2 What types of intelligence did Gardner and Sternberg identify? p. 209 | |
| 7.3 What was Alfred Binet's major contribution to psychology? p. 211 | |
| 7.4 What does IQ mean, and how was it originally calculated? p. 212 | |
| 7.5 What is the Stanford-Binet Intelligence Scale? p. 212 | |
| 7.6 What did David Wechsler's tests provide that the Stanford-Binet did not? p. 213 | |
| 7.7 What is meant by the terms *reliability, validity*, and *standardization*? p. 213 | |
| 7.8 What are the ranges of IQ scores that are considered average, superior, and in the range of mental disability? p. 214 | |
| 7.9 According to the Terman study, how do gifted people differ from the general population? p. 215 | |
| 7.10 What two criteria must a person meet to be classified as mentally disabled? p. 215 | |

7.11 What do intelligence tests predict well? p. 216

7.12 What are some of the abuses of intelligence tests? p. 216

7.13 How does the nature–nurture controversy apply to intelligence? p. 217

7.14 What is behavioural genetics, and what are the primary methods used in the field today? p. 217

7.15 How do twin studies support the view that intelligence is inherited? p. 218

7.16 What kinds of evidence suggest that IQ is changeable rather than fixed? p. 218

7.17 What are Herrnstein and Murray's controversial views on race and IQ? p. 219

7.18 What are the personal components of emotional intelligence? p. 220

7.19 What are the interpersonal components of emotional intelligence? p. 220

7.20 What is imagery? p. 222

| | |
|---|---|
| 7.21 What are concepts, and how are they formed? p. 223 | |
| 7.22 What are three problem-solving techniques, and how are they used? p. 224 | |
| 7.23 What are the two major impediments to problem solving? p. 226 | |
| 7.24 What is creativity, and what tests have been designed to measure it? p. 227 | |
| 7.25 What are the five important components of language? p. 229 | |
| 7.26 How do learning theory and the nativist position explain the acquisition of language? p. 231 | |
| 7.27 How does language in trained chimpanzees differ from human language? p. 234 | |
| 7.28 What is the linguistic relativity hypothesis, and is it supported by research? p. 235 | |
| | |
| | |

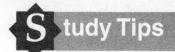
## Study Tips

## Try It

Learn to study more effectively and improve your memory with these tips and practical exercises.

## Anxiety Interferes with Performance

Do you freeze up on exams, worried that you won't do well? We can turn one exam into a "do or die" catastrophic situation. Yes, we should try our best, but we are not doomed for life if we fail at something. Perhaps the following examples will help you see a failure for what it is, just one more step in the process of life.

- Einstein was four years old before he could speak and seven before he could read.

- Isaac Newton did poorly in grade school.

- Beethoven's music teacher once said of him, "As a composer he is hopeless."

- When Thomas Edison was a boy, his teachers told him he was too stupid to learn anything.

- Woolworth got a job in a dry goods store when he was 21, but his employers would not let him wait on a customer because he "didn't have enough sense."

- A newspaper editor fired Walt Disney because he had "no good ideas."

- Leo Tolstoy flunked out of college.

- Louis Pasteur was rated as "mediocre" in chemistry when he attended college.

- Abraham Lincoln entered the Black Hawk War as a captain and came out as a private.

- Winston Churchill failed the sixth grade.

Failures mean very little in the big picture of our lives. It is just important that we keep trying.

## Problem-Solving Technique

Try the technique outlined below on a problem in your own life.

| Technique | Your Problem |
|---|---|
| **Stage 1** Describe problem | |
| **Stage 2** Generate possible solutions | |
| **Stage 3** Evaluate solutions | |
| **Stage 4** Try solutions, evaluate results | |
| **Revisions** Try new solutions, evaluate results | |

# Study Habits That Aid Memory

All learners are not created equal. Still, there are habits and skills that can aid the memory process when learning new material such as that in your text.

1. **Organization**—It is best to organize the material you are committing to memory in a meaningful way. When you go looking for it, it will be easier to find.

2. **Overlearning**—Don't stop studying when you think you know the material. Go over it again and again until it feels like you more than know it. You will remember more when test time comes if you overlearn the material.

3. **Spaced versus Massed Practice**—Study a little bit every day for the duration of your course. For example, if you study every day for 0.5 hours, you will be more likely to recall the material than if you study 3.5 hours (i.e., the same massed time) once per week.

4. **Active Learning versus Rereading**—Be on a quest for answers when you approach the material. Seek to actively learn the answers to your questions as opposed to passively reading the text. It will make a difference at recall time.

## Find Your EQ

Emotional intelligence may be just as important to success in your academic career as your actual academic skills. Take this short test to assess your EQ. Check one response for each statement.

1. I am always aware of even subtle feelings as I have them.

___Always ___Usually ___Sometimes

___Rarely ___Never

2. I can delay gratification in pursuit of my goals instead of getting carried away by impulse.

___Always ___Usually ___Sometimes

___Rarely ___Never

3. Instead of giving up in the face of setbacks or disappointments, I stay hopeful and optimistic.

___Always ___Usually ___Sometimes

___Rarely ___Never

4. My keen sense of others' feelings makes me compassionate about their plight.

___Always ___Usually ___Sometimes

___Rarely ___Never

5. I can sense the pulse of a group or relationship and state unspoken feelings.

___Always ___Usually ___Sometimes

___Rarely ___Never

6. I can soothe or contain distressing feelings so that they don't keep me from doing the things I need to do.

___Always ___Usually ___Sometimes

___Rarely ___Never

Score your responses as follows:
Always = 4 points, Usually = 3 points, Sometimes = 2 points, Rarely = 1 point, Never = 0 points. The closer your total number of points is to 24, the higher your EQ probably is.

After studying the text and completing the Study Guide activities, answer these questions to determine if you need to review any areas before your exam.

1. The first intelligence test was developed by ____ as a means of identifying children who could not benefit from regular education.
   a. Binet
   b. Terman
   c. Stanford
   d. Wechsler

2. On an intelligence test, a 5-year-old child is able to answer the questions that the average 6-year-old can answer. The child's IQ is:
   a. 120.
   b. 125.
   c. 100.
   d. 95.

3. According to the original formula for IQ, if a person's mental age and chronological age were equal, IQ would be:
   a. zero.
   b. one.
   c. 100.
   d. 110.

4. The Wechsler scales are made up of two basic subtest divisions. They are the _____ and the _____ divisions.
   a. verbal; performance
   b. verbal; information
   c. performance; mathematical
   d. vocabulary; information

5. A test is said to be reliable if it:
   a. measures what it says it measures.
   b. gives consistent results when a person is retested.
   c. tests many different abilities.
   d. does not show racial and ethnic differences in scores.

6. If a test measures what it is supposed to measure, it is said to be:
   a. reliable.
   b. valid.
   c. culture-free.
   d. cognitively complex.

7. In order to standardize a test,
   a. compose items that reflect the knowledge and behaviours of experts in the quality being tested.
   b. give subjects half the test items on one occasion and the other half on another, and compare consistency.
   c. arrange items to reflect the predictions of a psychological theory.
   d. administer it to a large number of people who represent the population for which the test was designed, and examine their scores.

8. What is the average IQ score in the Stanford-Binet and Wechsler?
   a. 50
   b. 75
   c. 100
   d. 150

9. What myths about gifted people did Terman's study disprove?
   a. Mentally superior people are likely to be physically inferior.
   b. There's a thin line between genius and madness.
   c. Gifted people don't have common sense.
   d. All of the above

10. Who was the theorist who suggested that the behaviours considered to be intelligent have a common factor called "general intelligence"?
    a. Sternberg
    b. Spearman
    c. Binet
    d. Terman

11. According to Sternberg's triarchic theory of intelligence, behaviour that permits people to adapt to the demands of their environment is intelligence called:
    a. contextual.
    b. experiential.
    c. componential.
    d. metacomponents.

12. Sternberg's model of intelligence differs from the traditional models in that Sternberg believes that:
    a. intelligence is inherited.
    b. intelligence includes how people function in the real world.
    c. IQ tests are biased toward minorities.
    d. there is only one kind of intelligence.

13. IQ tests are:
    a. good predictors of success in school.
    b. good predictors of success in life but not in school.
    c. good predictors of motivation but not success.
    d. poorly correlated with any other measure of achievement.

14. Many psychologists believe that the IQ tests in current use are:
    a. culture-free.
    b. unreliable.
    c. biased in favour of minorities.
    d. biased in favour of the white middle class.

15. Studies have found a stronger relationship between IQ scores of adopted children and their _____ parents than with their _____ parents.
    a. adoptive; grand-
    b. biological; grand-
    c. biological; adoptive
    d. adoptive; biological

16. The best way to assess the relative contributions of heredity and environment is to:
    a. compare identical and fraternal twins.
    b. study identical twins who have been separated at birth and reared apart.
    c. study fraternal twins who have been separated at birth and reared apart.
    d. study children who were adopted at birth by comparing them to their biological and adoptive parents.

17. In Emotional Intelligence, managing emotions means to:
    a. give free rein to every feeling and impulse.
    b. express emotions in an appropriate manner.
    c. suppress our emotions in public.
    d. display only positive emotional moods.

18. With the _____ approach to problem-solving, you try various solutions until, perhaps, one will work.
    a. analogy
    b. algorithm
    c. heuristic
    d. trial-and-error

19. Using a mental set to solve a problem refers to our tendency to:
    a. stand back from a problem.
    b. use set procedures that guarantee success.
    c. use techniques that worked in the past.
    d. use means–end analysis.

20. The tendency to view an object in terms of its familiar usage is defined as:
    a. mental set.
    b. incubation.
    c. functional fixedness.
    d. algorithmic perception.

21. The ability to generate novel solutions to problems, characterized by originality, ingenuity, and flexibility, is referred to as:
    a. creativity.
    b. intelligence.
    c. algorithmic activity.
    d. heuristic thinking.

22. A 2-year-old calling every car, bus, truck, and motorcycle a "car" illustrates:
    a. overregularization.
    b. overextension.
    c. mental combinations.
    d. mental representation.

23. Which of the following factors contributes to creativity?
    a. originality
    b. dependency
    c. conformity
    d. inhibition

24. Which of the following is an interpersonal component of Emotional Intelligence?
    a. being self-motivated.
    b. an ability to postpone immediate gratification.
    c. managing our inner feelings about others.
    d. an ability to handle relationships.

25. Peters (1995) and Winston (1996) have challenged the allegations of J. Philippe Rushton that races could be ranked in order of intelligence. They questioned:

    a. Rushton's methodology.
    b. the accuracy of his measurement.
    c. whether the studies actually tested intelligence.
    d. all of the above.

26. A study of children conceived during WWII (Eyeferth, 1961) showed that:
    a. Rushton's methodology was corrupt.
    b. having a black father conferred a measurable IQ advantage.
    c. having a white father conferred a measurable IQ advantage.
    d. having a white father conferred no measurable IQ advantage at all.

| Question Number | Answer | Learning Objective | Explanation for application questions |
|---|---|---|---|
| 1. | a. | 7.3 | |
| 2. | a. | 7.4 | $IQ = \dfrac{\text{mental age}}{\text{chronological age}} \times 100$ |
| 3. | c. | 7.4 | $\dfrac{6}{5} \times 100 = 120$ $\dfrac{\text{mental age}}{\text{chronological age}} = 1 \times 100 = 100$ |
| 4. | a. | 7.5 | Wechsler scales are the verbal and performance. |
| 5. | b. | 7.7 | |
| 6. | b. | 7.7 | |
| 7. | d. | 7.7 | Standardization is defined in response d. |
| 8. | c. | 7.8 | The average IQ is 100 for both Stanford-Binet and Wechsler. |
| 9. | d. | 7.9 | Terman disproved all three of the myths listed in the responses. |
| 10. | b. | 7.1 | Spearman believed there was a common factor "g." |
| 11. | a. | 7.2 | Sternberg's theory consisted of componential (IQ score), experiential (insight), and contextual (common sense). |
| 12. | b. | 7.9 | Sternberg was interested in how a person functioned in the environment. |
| 13. | a. | 7.11 | IQ tests are similar to school exams, so IQ test performance can predict school success. |
| 14. | d. | 7.12 | Most IQ tests use the vocabulary of the white middle class and therefore favour them. |
| 15. | c. | 7.13 | IQ scores are closer in blood relatives as compared with non-related people living together. |
| 16. | b. | 7.15 | |
| 17. | b. | 7.18 | |
| 18. | d. | 7.22 | |
| 19. | c. | 7.23 | A mental set interferes with our openness to new ideas because it is a focus on techniques that worked in the past. |
| 20. | c. | 7.23 | |
| 21. | a. | 7.24 | The question describes creativity. |
| 22. | b. | 7.27 | Inappropriately applying the grammatical rules for forming plurals and past tenses to irregular nouns. |
| 23. | a. | 7.24 | |
| 24. | d. | 7.19 | |
| 25. | d. | 7.17 | Guelph University researchers brought forward major concerns over Rushton's research |
| 26. | d. | 7.17 | The results were obtained by comparing IQs of children with black fathers with children with white fathers. |

# Glossary for Text Language Enhancement

Students identified the following words from the text as needing more explanation. This page can be cut out, folded in half, and used as a bookmark for this chapter.

| term | definition |
| --- | --- |
| legacy | something passed on by a predecessor |
| genius | very intelligent |
| prominent | important |
| labelled | said to be |
| dunce | not smart |
| tap | connect with |
| dexterity | ability |
| formulated | put together |
| deficient | not as good as expected |
| flaw | mistake |
| highly regarded | thought highly of |
| gifted | very intelligent |
| height | how tall someone is |
| cluster | group together |
| infallible | always works correctly |
| whether | either |
| disentangle | separate |
| reared | raised |
| gap | difference |
| impulse | sudden idea |
| free flowing | not structured |
| hallmark | important quality |
| dimmer | not sharp |
| retrieve | recall, remember |
| stored | held in brain |
| grasp | understand |
| fuzzy | not clear |
| embodies | contains |
| mundane | common everyday experience or thing |
| water lily | type of plant that grows in ponds |
| hampered | held back |
| broader | applies to more settings |
| praise | kind words of approval |

# Thinking Critically

## Evaluation

Which of the theories of intelligence best fits your notion of intelligence? Why?

## Point/Counterpoint

Prepare an argument supporting each of the following positions:

a. Intelligence tests should be used in schools.

b. Intelligence tests should not be used in schools.

## Psychology in Your Life

Give several examples of how tools of thinking (imagery and concepts) and problem-solving strategies (algorithms and heuristics) can be applied in your educational and personal life.

| | |
|:---:|:---:|
| *g* factor | deviation score |
| primary mental abilities | Wechsler Adult Intelligence Scale |
| structure of intellect | reliability |
| triarchic theory of intelligence | validity |
| intelligence quotient (IQ) | longitudinal study |
| norms | standardization |
| Stanford-Binet Intelligence Scale | mental disability |

| | |
|---|---|
| A test score calculated by comparing an individual's score to the scores of others of the same age on whom the test's norms were formed. | Spearman's term for a general intellectual ability that underlies all mental operations to some degree. |
| An individual intelligence test for adults that yields separate verbal and performance (non-verbal) IQ scores as well as an overall IQ score. | According to Thurstone, seven relatively distinct abilities that singularly or in combination are involved in all intellectual activities. |
| The ability of a test to yield nearly the same score when the same people are tested and then retested on the same test or an alternative form of the test. | The model proposed by Guilford consisting of 180 different intellectual abilities, which involve all of the possible combinations of the three dimensions of intellect—mental operations, contents, and products. |
| The ability of a test to measure what it is intended to measure. | Sternberg's theory that intelligence consists of three parts—the componential, the contextual, and the experiential. |
| A type of developmental study in which the same group of participants is followed and measured at different ages. | An index of intelligence originally derived by dividing mental age by chronological age and then multiplying by 100. |
| The establishment of norms for comparing the scores of people who take a test in the future; administering tests using a prescribed procedure. | Standards based on the range of test scores of a large group of people who are selected to provide the bases of comparison for those who take the test later. |
| Subnormal intelligence reflected by an IQ below 70 and by adaptive functioning severely deficient for one's age. | An individually administered IQ test for those aged 2 to 23; Lewis Terman's adaptation of the Binet-Simon Scale. |

| | |
|---|---|
| mainstreaming | adoption study method |
| culture-fair intelligence test | imagery |
| nature–nurture controversy | concept |
| behavioural genetics | prototype |
| twin study method | exemplars |
| identical and fraternal twins | trial and error |
| heritability | algorithm |

| | |
|---|---|
| A method researchers use to study the relative effects of heredity and environment on behaviour and ability in children adopted shortly after birth, by comparing them to their biological and adoptive parents. | Educating mentally disabled students in regular rather than special schools by placing them in regular classes for part of the day or having special classrooms in regular schools. |
| The representation in the mind of a sensory experience—visual, auditory, gustatory, motor, olfactory, or tactile. | An intelligence test that uses questions that will not penalize those whose culture differs from that of the middle or upper classes. |
| A label that represents a class or group of objects, people, or events sharing common characteristics or attributes. | The debate over whether intelligence and other traits are primarily the result of heredity or environment. |
| The example that embodies the most common and typical features of a concept. | A field of research that investigates the relative effects of heredity and environment on behaviour and ability. |
| The individual instance of a concept that we have stored in memory from our own experience. | Studying identical and fraternal twins to determine the relative effects of heredity and environment on a variety of characteristics. |
| An approach to problem solving in which one solution after another is tried in no particular order until a workable solution is found. | Twins with identical genes; monozygotic twins. The second term refers to twins who are not more alike genetically than ordinary brothers and sisters; dizygotic twins. |
| A systematic, step-by-step procedure, such as a mathematical formula, that guarantees a solution to a problem of a certain type if the algorithm is appropriate and executed properly. | An index of the degree to which a characteristic is estimated to be influenced by heredity. |

| | |
|---|---|
| heuristic | creativity |
| working backward | divergent thinking |
| means–end analysis | psycholinguistics |
| functional fixedness | morphemes |
| mental set | syntax |
| semantics | linguistic relativity hypothesis |
| emotional intelligence | cognition |

| | |
|---|---|
| The ability to produce original, appropriate, and valuable ideas and/or solutions to problems. | A problem-solving method that offers a promising way to attack a problem and arrive at a solution, although it does not guarantee success. |
| Producing one or more possible ideas, answers, or solutions to a problem rather than a single, correct response. | A heuristic strategy in which a person discovers the steps needed to solve a problem by refining the desired goal and working backward to the current condition. |
| The study of how language is acquired, produced, and used, and how the sounds and symbols of language are translated into meaning. | A heuristic problem-solving strategy in which the current position is compared with the desired goal, and a series of steps are formulated and taken to close the gap between them. |
| The smallest units of meaning in a language. | The failure to use familiar objects in novel ways to solve problems because of a tendency to view objects only in terms of their customary functions. |
| The aspect of grammar that specifies the rules for arranging and combining words to form phrases and sentences. | The tendency to apply a familiar strategy to the solution of a problem without carefully considering the special requirements of the problem. |
| The notion that the language a person speaks largely determines the nature of that person's thoughts. | The meaning or the study of meaning derived from morphemes, words, and sentences. |
| The mental processes involved in acquiring, storing, retrieving, and using information. | A type of intelligence that includes an awareness of and an ability to manage one's own emotions, the ability to motivate oneself, empathy, and the ability to handle relationships successfully. |

| | |
|---|---|
| phonemes | surface structure |
| overextension | |
| underextension | |
| telegraphic speech | |
| overregularization | |
| babbling | |
| deep structure | |

| | |
|---|---|
| The literal words of a sentence that we speak, write, or sign. | The smallest units of sound in a spoken languge. |
| | The act of using a word, on the basis of some shared feature, to apply to a broader range of objects than appropriate. |
| | Restricting the use of a word to only a few, rather than to all, members of a class of objects. |
| | Short sentences that follow a strict word order and contain only essential content words. |
| | The act of inappropriately applying the grammatical rules for forming plurals and past tenses to irregular nouns and verbs. |
| | Vocalization of the basic speech sounds (phonemes), which begins between the ages of 4 months and 6 months. |
| | The underlying meaning of a sentence. |

# 8

# DEVELOPMENT

This outline provides a way to organize your notes from both the text and the lecture. It will also serve as a review for the exam.

| Module 8.1 Developmental Psychology: Basic Issues and Methodology | 1. Controversial Issues in Developmental Psychology |
| --- | --- |
| | 2. Approaches to Studying Developmental Change |
| |     a. Longitudinal Study (see next page) |
| |     b. Cross-Sectional Study |

## A Comparison of Longitudinal and Cross-Sectional Studies

**Longitudinal Study**
The same group of subjects is studied on several occasions over an extended period of time to determine age changes on particular characteristics.

| First Study 1992 | Second Study 1994 | Third Study 1997 | Fourth Study 2000 |
|---|---|---|---|
| Subjects 1 year old | Same subjects at 3 years | Same subjects at 6 years | Same subjects at 9 years |

The same group is studied over a period of 8 years.

**Cross-Sectional Study**
Group of subjects of different ages are studied at one point in time and compared on particular characteristics.

| Group One | Group Two | Group Three | Group Four |
|---|---|---|---|
| Subjects 1 year old | Subjects 3 years old | Subjects 6 years old | Subjects 9 years old |

All groups are studied in 1999

---

**Module 8.2 Heredity and Prenatal Development**

1. The Mechanism of Heredity: Genes and Chromosomes

   a. Dominant and Recessive Genes

2. The Stages of Prenatal Development: Unfolding According to Plan

   a. Multiple Births

      • Identical Twins (monozygotic)

      • Fraternal Twins (dizygotic)

3. Negative Influences on Prenatal Development: Sabotaging Nature's Plan

   • The Hazard of Drugs

   • Newborns at High Risk

| Module 8.3 Physical Development and Learning | 1. The Neonate |
|---|---|
| | • Reflexes: Built-In Responses |
| | 2. Perceptual Development in Infancy |
| | • Vision: What Newborns Can See |
| | 3. Learning in Infancy |
| | 4. Physical and Motor Development: Growing, Growing, Grown |
| | a. Infancy |
| | b. Puberty |
| | c. Middle Age |
| Module 8.4 The Cognitive Stages of Development: Climbing the Steps to Cognitive Maturity | 1. Piaget's Stages of Cognitive Development |
| | a. The Sensorimotor Stage (Birth to Age Two) |
| | b. The Preoperational Stage (Ages Two to Seven) |

| Conservation Task | Age of Acquisition | Original Presentation | Transformation |
|---|---|---|---|
| Number | 6–7 years | Are there the same number of pennies in each row? | Now are there the same number of pennies in each row, or does one row have more? |
| Liquid | 6–7 years | Is there the same amount of juice in each glass? | Now is there the same amount of juice in each glass, or does one have more? |
| Mass | 6–7 years | Is there the same amount of clay in each ball? | Now does each piece have the same amount of clay, or does one have more? |
| Area | 8–10 years | Does each of these two cows have the same amount of grass to eat? | Now does each cow have the same amount of grass to eat, or does one cow have more? |

c.  The Concrete Operations Stage (Ages 7 to 11 or 12)

d.  The Formal Operations Stage (Ages 11 or 12 and Beyond)

2.  An Evaluation of Piaget's Contribution

3.  Intellectual Capacity During Early, Middle, and Late Adulthood

| | |
|---|---|
| Module 8.5 Socialization and Social Relationships | 1.  Erikson's Theory of Psychosocial Development<br><br>• Psychosocial Stages<br><br>a.  Stage 1: Basic Trust versus Basic Mistrust (Birth to 12 Months)<br><br>b.  Stage 2: Autonomy versus Shame and Doubt (Ages One to Three)<br><br>c.  Stage 3: Initiative versus Guilt (Ages Three to Six)<br><br>d.  Stage 4: Industry versus Inferiority (Ages Six to Puberty)<br><br>e.  Stage 5: Identity versus Role Confusion (Adolescence)<br><br>f.  Stage 6: Intimacy versus Isolation (Young Adulthood)<br><br>g.  Stage 7: Generativity versus Stagnation (Middle Adulthood)<br><br>h.  Stage 8: Ego Integrity versus Despair (Late Adulthood) |

2. The Parents' Role in the Socialization Process

   a. Attachment in Infant Monkeys

   b. The Necessity for Love

   c. The Development of Attachment in Humans

      • Separation Anxiety

   d. Ainsworth's Study of Attachment

      i.  Secure Attachment

      ii. Avoidant Attachment

      iii. Resistant Attachment

      iv. Disorganized/Disoriented Attachment

   e. Parenting Styles

      i. Authoritarian

      ii. Authoritative

      iii. Permissive

| | |
|---|---|
| | 3. Peer Relationships.<br><br>    a. Adolescent Egocentrism: On Centre Stage, Unique, and Indestructible<br><br>    b. The Development of Physical Aggression<br><br>4. Kohlberg's Theory of Moral Development<br><br>    a. Levels of Moral Reasoning<br><br>        i. Preconventional<br><br>        ii. Conventional<br><br>        iii. Postconventional<br><br>    b. The Development of Moral Reasoning<br><br>    c. Research on Kohlberg's Theory |
| Module 8.6 Special Concerns in Later Adulthood | 1. Fitness and Aging<br><br><br>2. Terminal Illness and Death<br><br>    a. Kübler-Ross<br><br><br>    b. Bereavement |
| Apply It! | Teenage Pregnancy: The Consequences for Mother and Child<br><br>Preventing Pregnancy and Cultural Contradictions |

# Chapter Learning Objective Questions

Answer the following questions in the space provided and check your answers on the page numbers listed.

| | |
|---|---|
| 8.1 What are two types of studies that developmental psychologists use to investigate age-related changes? p. 246 | |
| 8.2 How are hereditary traits transmitted? p. 248 | |
| 8.3 When are dominant or recessive genes expressed in a person? p. 248 | |
| 8.4 What are the three stages of prenatal development? p. 250 | |
| 8.5 What are some negative influences on prenatal development, and when is their impact greatest? p. 251 | |
| 8.6 What are the perceptual abilities of the newborn? p. 253 | |
| 8.7 What types of learning occur in the first few days of life? p. 254 | |
| 8.8 What physical changes occur during puberty? p. 254 | |
| 8.9 What are the physical changes associated with middle age? p. 255 | |
| 8.10 What were Piaget's beliefs regarding stages of cognitive development? p. 257 | |

8.11 What is Piaget's sensorimotor stage? p. 257

8.12 What cognitive limitations characterize a child's thinking during the preoperational stage? p. 258

8.13 What cognitive abilities do children acquire during the concrete operations stage? p. 259

8.14 What new capability characterizes the formal operations stage? p. 259

8.15 In general, can adults look forward to an increase or decrease in intellectual performance from their 20s to their 60s? p. 261

8.16 What is Erikson's theory of psychosocial development? p. 262

8.17 What did Harlow's studies reveal about maternal deprivation and attachment in infant monkeys? p. 264

8.18 When does the infant have a strong attachment to the mother? p. 265

8.19 What are the four attachment patterns identified in infants? p. 265

8.20 What are the three parenting styles discussed by Baumrind, and which did she find most effective? p. 266

| 8.21 How do peers contribute to the socialization process? p. 267 | |
|---|---|
| 8.22 What are Kohlberg's three levels of moral reasoning? p. 269 | |
| 8.23 What do cross-cultural studies reveal about the universality of Kohlberg's theory? p. 270 | |
| 8.24 According to Kübler-Ross, what stages do terminally ill patients experience as they come to terms with death? p. 272 | |
| | |
| | |
| | |
| | |
| | |

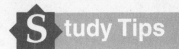 

Learn to study more effectively and improve your memory with these tips and practical exercises.

## Effective Note-Taking During Class

1. **Review the textbook chapter before class.**
   Instructors often design a lecture based on the assumption that you have read the chapter before class. You can take notes more easily if you already have some idea of the material.

2. **Bring your favourite note-taking tools to class.**
   Make sure you have pencils, pens, highlighter markers, paper, note cards, or whatever materials you find useful.

3. **Sit as close to the instructor as possible.**
   You will have fewer distractions while taking your notes.

4. **Arrive at class early.**
   Relax and get your brain "tuned-up" to the subject by reviewing your notes from the previous class.

5. **Picture yourself up front with the instructor.**
   The more connected you feel to the material and the instructor, the more you will understand and remember the topic.

6. **Let go of judgments and debates.**
   Focus on understanding what the instructor is saying because that is what you will find on the test. Do not get distracted by evaluating the instructor's lecture style, appearance, or strange habits. When you hear something you disagree with, make a quick note of it and then let it go.

7. **Be active in class.**
   It is the best way to stay awake in class! Volunteer for demonstrations. Join in class discussions.

8. **Relate the topic to an interest of yours.**
   We remember things that interest us.

9. **Watch for clues of what is important.**
   - repetition
   - summary statements
   - information written on the board
   - information the instructor takes directly from his or her notes

Notice what interests the instructor.

## Testing Child Development

Find a child who is between the ages of 3 and 5 and observe them trying the following tasks.

1. Locate three glasses, two the exact same shape and size, and the third one a noticeably different shape but able to hold about the same amount of liquid.

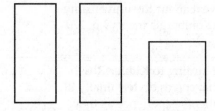

2. Fill the identical glasses with liquid up to the same level.
3. Ask the child which glass has more in it.
4. With the child watching, pour the liquid from one of the glasses into the glass of a different shape.
5. Ask the child which glass now has more in it.

> What principle of Piaget have you demonstrated?

You can do further experiments by showing a child two balls of clay and then flattening one. Ask the child which ball of clay is bigger. You can also ask a child which sandwich is bigger, a half sandwich cut into three pieces or an uncut whole sandwich. (You must show the child the sandwiches.)

answer to Piaget question: conservation

## Battle Procrastination

You might do fine when you study, but just to get to the books can be a challenge. How do you battle a common problem, procrastination? Some tips include the following:

1. Identify the environmental cues that habitually interfere with your studying.
2. Schedule your study time and reinforce yourself for adhering to your schedule.
3. Get started. Just open the book and get moving. That's the hard part.
4. Use visualization of negative consequences if you don't get the work done.
5. Become better at estimating how long it takes to complete an assignment.
6. Avoid jumping to another task when you reach the difficult part of an assignment.
7. Avoid preparation overkill. Don't plan for hours and then work for minutes

After studying the text and completing the Study Guide activities, answer these questions to determine if you need to review any areas before your exam.

1. Which of the following issues is most closely associated with the nature–nurture controversy?
   a. To what extent are personal characteristics stable over time?
   b. To what degree do heredity and environment influence development?
   c. Is it ethical to compare the development of humans and animals?
   d. Is development continuous or does it occur in stages?

2. A gene is said to be recessive when:
   a. it is covered by the other gene in the chromosome.
   b. its influence is obscured if it is paired with a dominant gene.
   c. it is smaller than the dominant gene.
   d. it does not appear in the individual's genotype.

3. Which of the following is not a stage of prenatal development?
   a. period of the fetus
   b. period of the zygote
   c. period of the ovum
   d. period of the embryo

4. What are some negative influences on prenatal development?
   a. certain prescription and nonprescription drugs
   b. poor maternal nutrition
   c. maternal infections and illnesses
   d. all of the above

5. A researcher who compares the level of education in groups of different ages to see the influence of education on successful aging is conducting a:
   a. genetic study
   b. longitudinal study
   c. difference study
   d. cross-sectional study

6. Pick the response that best describes the sensory ability of the newborn.
   a. Not all of the newborn's senses are functional at birth.
   b. The neonate has preferences for certain sounds.
   c. The neonate does not have taste preference yet.
   d. All of the above.

7. What type of learning occurs in the first few days of life?
   a. habituation
   b. classical conditioning
   c. operant conditioning and observational learning
   d. all of the above

8. All of the following are secondary sex characteristics EXCEPT:
   a. breast development in females.
   b. underarm and pubic hair in both sexes.
   c. ovaries in females.
   d. voice change in males.

9. Harlow's classic research with infant monkeys has illustrated the importance of which of the following in early development?
   a. contact comfort
   b. regular feeding
   c. freedom to explore
   d. a stimulating environment

10. What are the four attachment patterns?
    a. tight, loose, fragmented, solid
    b. reserved, fearful, schema, and conceptual
    c. secure, resistant, avoidant, and disorganized/disoriented
    d. dependent, independent, marginal, main

11. According to Piaget what is the major accomplishment of the sensorimotor stage?
    a. abstract thinking
    b. egocentrism
    c. centration
    d. object permanence

12. What cognitive limitation characterizes a child's thinking during the preoperational stage?
    a. egocentrism
    b. centration
    c. lack of conservation and reversibility
    d. all of the above

13. During the stage of concrete operations children:
    a. understand the concept of reversibility.
    b. do not yet understand the concept of conservation.
    c. are able to solve abstract problems.
    d. none of the above.

14. What new capability characterizes the formal operations stage?
    a. concrete thinking
    b. conservation
    c. reversibility
    d. abstract thinking

15. Which of the following statements would apply to an adult education class?
    a. Since all of the students will have obtained formal operational thought, relevance will be crucial.
    b. It is possible that many of these adults may not have attained the skills of formal operational thought.
    c. Probably fewer than 15 percent of the class can solve theoretical problems.
    d. none of the above

16. Adolescents who feel they are protected from misfortune are experiencing a
    a. personal fable
    b. cognitive impairment
    c. moral dilemma
    d. pretend audience

17. At Kohlberg's conventional level, the morality of a particular action is determined by whether or not the:
    a. actions help the individual to satisfy personal needs.
    b. individual's actions uphold self-chosen ethical standards.
    c. individual's actions will be approved by other persons.
    d. individual's actions result in punishment.

18. Carol Gilligan criticized Kohlberg for:
    a. concentrating too much on moral reasoning and too little on moral behaviour.
    b. claiming that his moral stages apply to people in all cultures.
    c. having underestimated the percentage of people who reach the postconventional level.
    d. having a theory that is sex-biased.

19. Erikson's theory emphasizes:
    a. a person's relationship to the social and cultural environment.
    b. the type of logic that underlies thought processes.
    c. life and its inherent rewards and punishments.
    d. active mental processes.

20. According to Baumrind what are three parenting styles?
    a. aristocratic, formal, and humanistic
    b. authoritarian, permissive, and authoritative
    c. formal, informal, and inconsistent
    d. easy, difficult, and slow-to-warm-up

21. How do peers contribute to the socialization process?
    a. modelling and reinforcing appropriate behaviours
    b. punishing inappropriate behaviour
    c. providing an objective measure for children to evaluate their own abilities
    d. all of the above

22. Erik Erikson would be most likely to say that one of the problems resulting from adolescent drug use is that it:
    a. interferes with the task of identity formation.
    b. fosters a sense of guilt and inferiority.
    c. is a threat to health and safety.
    d. is an early symptom of emotional disorders.

23. In late adulthood, regular exercise:
    a. is not desirable.
    b. can greatly increase energy and fitness.
    c. increases the risk of heart attack.
    d. is not as important as at earlier ages.

24. Which of the following is the correct sequence of Kübler-Ross's stages of dying?
    a. denial, depression, anger, bargaining, acceptance
    b. depression, denial, anger, bargaining, acceptance
    c. anger, denial, bargaining, depression, acceptance
    d. denial, anger, bargaining, depression, acceptance

| Question Number | Answer | Learning Objective | Explanation for application questions |
|---|---|---|---|
| 1. | b. | 8.1 | |
| 2. | b. | 8.3 | A recessive gene is expressed when it is paired with another recessive gene. |
| 3. | c. | 8.4 | |
| 4. | d. | 8.5 | All of the responses are true. |
| 5. | d. | 8.1 | |
| 6. | b. | 8.6 | All of the newborn's senses are functional at birth. |
| 7. | d. | 8.7 | All of the responses are true. |
| 8. | c. | 8.8 | |
| 9. | a. | 8.17 | |
| 10. | c. | 8.19 | |
| 11. | d. | 8.11 | Object permanence is the major accomplishment of this stage. |
| 12. | d. | 8.12 | All responses are correct. |
| 13. | a. | 8.13 | Children at the concrete operations stage become able to decentre their thinking and to understand the concepts of reversibility and conservation. |
| 14. | d. | 8.14 | Abstract problem solving is the most significant cognitive development. |
| 15. | b. | 8.15 | Not everyone reaches the formal operations stage. |
| 16. | a. | 8.14 | |
| 17. | c. | 8.22 | |
| 18. | d. | | |
| 19. | a. | 8.15 | Erikson's stages are called psychosocial and emphasize our relationship to society. |
| 20. | b. | 8.20 | |
| 21. | d. | 8.21 | All responses are correct. |
| 22. | a. | 8.16 | |
| 23. | b. | 8.24 | |
| 24. | d. | 8.24 | |

Students identified the following words from the text as needing more explanation. This page can be cut out, folded in half, and used as a bookmark for this chapter.

| term | definition |
| --- | --- |
| lush | many plants |
| squeal | high-pitched sound |
| edible | can be eaten |
| squat | sit on the back of legs |
| slaughtered | killed |
| lifespan | through one's life |
| eras | periods of time |
| transmission | act of passing on characteristics by heredity |
| Genome | study chromosomes |
| gene pool | the possible genetic combinations available in a particular place |
| stillbirth | baby born dead |
| stroke | pet |
| fixate | stare |
| milestones | significant events |
| culminates | ends |
| comprehensive | detailed |
| systematically | done in steps |
| egocentrism | thinking of the world only from your own point of view |
| inanimate | without life |
| obstacles | things that block your way |
| monumental | important |
| conventional wisdom | commonly accepted belief |
| downhill | a state of decline |
| expertise | special skill or knowledge |
| mistrust | not trusting |
| resolution | completion, to finish |
| mischief | bad behaviour |
| bonding | mutual connection |
| stare fixedly | look without moving |
| mesh | wire fencing |
| crib | bed for babies |
| draped | covered |
| stare | look |
| dwarfism | very small size |
| gazes | looks |
| peer group | people the same age as you |
| delinquency | adolescent illegal activity |

| term | definition |
|---|---|
| impulsive | acts quickly without thinking |
| indestructibility | cannot be destroyed |
| dilemmas | problems with several answers possible, difficult to pick one |
| contemplate | think about |
| inconsolably | not to be comforted |

# Thinking Critically

## Evaluation

In your opinion, do Erikson's psychosocial stages for adolescence and early adulthood accurately represent the major conflicts of these periods of life? Explain.

## Point/Counterpoint

Prepare an argument supporting each of these positions:

a.  Physical development peaks in the early adult years and declines thereafter.

b.  Physical development can be maintained throughout life.

## Psychology in Your Life

Using Erikson's theory, try to relate the first four stages of psychosocial development to your life.

Using Baumrind's scheme, classify the parenting style your mother and/or father used in rearing you.

a.  Cite examples of techniques they used that support your classification.

b.  Do you agree with Baumrind's conclusions about the effects of that parenting style on children? Explain.

| | |
|---|---|
| developmental psychology | dominant gene |
| nature–nurture controversy | recessive gene |
| longitudinal study | zygote |
| cross-sectional study | prenatal |
| genes | embryo |
| chromosomes | fetus |
| sex chromosomes | identical (monozygotic) twins |

| | |
|---|---|
| The gene that is expressed in the individual. | The study of how humans grow, develop, and change throughout the lifespan. |
| A gene that will not be expressed if paired with a dominant gene but will be expressed if paired with another recessive gene. | The debate concerning the relative influences of heredity and environment on development. |
| The first 2 weeks of development. | A type of developmental study in which the same group of individuals is followed and measured at different ages. |
| Occurring between conception and birth. | A type of developmental study in which researchers compare groups of individuals of different ages on certain characteristics to determine age-related differences. |
| The developing human organism during the period (week 3 through week 8) when the major systems, organs, and structures of the body develop. | Within the chromosomes, the segments of DNA that are the basic units for the transmission of hereditary traits. |
| The developing human organism during the period (week 9 until birth) of rapid growth and further development of the structures, organs, and systems of the body. | Rod-shaped structures, found in the nuclei of body cells, that contain all the genes and carry all the hereditary information. |
| Twins with exactly the same genes, who develop after one egg is fertilized by one sperm, and the zygote splits into two parts. | The 23rd pair of chromosomes, carrying the genes that determine one's sex and primary and secondary sex characteristics. |

| | |
|---|---|
| fraternal (dizygotic) twins | reflexes |
| teratogens | menopause |
| critical period | habituation |
| fetal alcohol spectrum syndrome | |
| low-birth-weight baby | |
| preterm infant | |
| neonate | |

| | |
|---|---|
| Inborn, unlearned, automatic responses to certain environmental stimuli. | Twins, no more alike genetically than ordinary siblings, who develop after two eggs are released during ovulation and fertilized by two different sperm. |
| The cessation of menstruation between ages 45 and 55 and signifying the end of reproductive capacity. | Harmful agents in the prenatal environment, which can have a negative impact on prenatal development and even cause birth defects. |
| A decrease in response or attention to a stimulus as an infant becomes accustomed to it. | A period that is so important to development that a harmful environmental influence can keep a bodily structure or behaviour from developing normally. |
| | A condition, caused by maternal alcohol intake during pregnancy, in which the baby is born mentally disabled, abnormally small, and with facial, organ, and limb abnormalities. |
| | A baby weighing less than 2.5 kilograms. |
| | An infant born before the 37th week. |
| | Newborn infant up to 1 month old. |

| | personal fable |
|---|---|
| puberty | conventional level of moral reasoning |
| adolescent growth spurt | preconventional level of moral reasoning |
| secondary sex characteristics | postconventional level of moral reasoning |
| menarche | identity versus role confusion |
| formal operations stage | intimacy versus isolation |
| imaginary audience | generativity versus stagnation |

| | |
|---|---|
| An exaggerated sense of personal uniqueness and indestructibility, which may be the basis of risk taking common during adolescence. | |
| Kohlberg's second level in which right and wrong are based on the internalized standard of others; "right" is whatever helps or is approved of by others, or whatever is consistent with the laws of society. | A period of rapid physical growth and change that culminates in sexual maturity. |
| Kohlberg's lowest level based on the physical consequences of an act; "right" is whatever avoids punishment or gains a reward. | A period of rapid physical growth that peaks in girls at about age 12 and in boys at about age 14. |
| Kohlberg's highest level in which moral reasoning involves weighing moral alternatives; "right" is whatever furthers basic human rights. | Those physical characteristics that are not directly involved in reproduction but distinguish the mature male from the mature female. |
| Erikson's fifth psychosocial stage, when adolescents need to establish their own identity and to form values to live by; failure can lead to an identity crisis. | The onset of menstruation. |
| Erikson's sixth psychosocial stage, when the young adult must establish intimacy in a relationship in order to avoid feeling a sense of isolation and loneliness. | Piaget's final stage of cognitive development, characterized by the ability to use logical reasoning in abstract situations. |
| Erikson's seventh psychosocial stage, occurring during middle age, when people become increasingly concerned with guiding the next generation rather than stagnating. | A belief of adolescents that they are or will be the focus of attention in social situations and that others will be as critical or approving as they are of themselves. |

| | |
|---|---|
| separation anxiety | preoperational stage |
| | conservation |
| schema | centration |
| assimilation | reversibility |
| accommodation | concrete operations stage |
| sensorimotor stage | formal operations stage |
| object permanence | ego integrity versus despair |

| | |
|---|---|
| Piaget's second stage of cognitive development (ages 2 to 7 years), characterized by rapid development of language and thinking governed by perception rather than logic. | The fear and distress shown by toddlers when their parent or caretaker leaves. |
| The concept that a given quantity of matter remains the same despite rearrangement or change in its appearance, as long as nothing has been added or taken away. | |
| The child's tendency during the preoperational stage to focus on only one dimension of a stimulus and ignore the other dimensions. | Piaget's term for a cognitive structure or concept used to identify and interpret information. |
| The realization, during the concrete operations stage, that any change occurring in the shape, position, or order of matter can be returned mentally to its original state. | The process by which new objects, events, experiences, or information are incorporated into existing schemas. |
| Piaget's third stage of cognitive development (ages 7 to 11 years), during which a child acquires the concepts of reversibility and conservation and is able to apply logical thinking to concrete objects. | The process by which existing schemas are modified and new schemas are created to incorporate new objects, events, experience, or information. |
| Piaget's fourth and final stage, characterized by the ability to apply logical thinking to abstract, verbal, and hypothetical situations, and to problems in the past, present, and future. | Piaget's first stage of cognitive development (ages birth to 2 years), culminating with the development of object permanence and the beginning of representational thought. |
| Erikson's eighth and final psychosocial stage, occurring during old age, when people look back on their lives with satisfaction or with regret about missed opportunities and mistakes. | The realization that objects continue to exist even when they are no longer perceived. |

| | |
|---|---|
| socialization | authoritative parents |
| psychosocial stages | permissive parents |
| basic trust versus basic mistrust | |
| autonomy versus shame and doubt | |
| initiative versus guilt | |
| industry versus inferiority | |
| authoritarian parents | |

| | |
|---|---|
| Parents who set high but realistic standards, reason with the child, enforce limits, and encourage open communication and independence. | The process of learning socially acceptable behaviours, attitudes, and values. |
| Parents who make few rules or demands and allow children to make their own decisions and control their own behaviour. | Erikson's eight developmental stages through the lifespan, each defined by a conflict that must be resolved satisfactorily in order for healthy personality development to occur. |
| | Erikson's first stage (ages birth to 1 year), when infants develop trust or mistrust based on the quality of care, love, and affection provided. |
| | Erikson's second stage (ages 1 to 3 years), when infants develop autonomy or shame based on how parents react to their expression of will and their wish to do things for themselves. |
| | Erikson's third stage (ages 3 to 6 years), when children develop a sense of initiative or guilt depending on how parents react to their initiation of play, their motor activities, and their questions. |
| | Erikson's fourth stage (ages 6 years to puberty), when children develop a sense of industry or inferiority based on how parents and teachers react to their efforts to undertake projects. |
| | Parents who make arbitrary rules, expect unquestioned obedience from their children, punish transgressions, and value obedience to authority. |

# 9

MOTIVATION
AND
EMOTION

2. Drive-Reduction Theory: Striving to Keep a Balanced Internal State

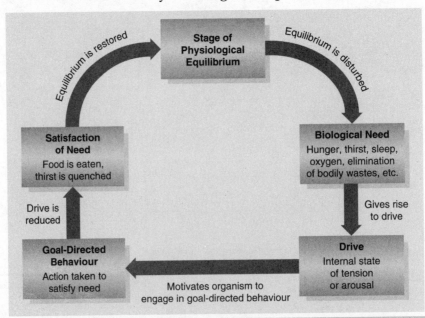

3. Arousal Theory: Striving for an Optimal Level of Arousal

    a. Stimulus Motives

    b. Arousal and Performance

4. Maslow's Hierarchy of Needs: Putting Our Needs in Order

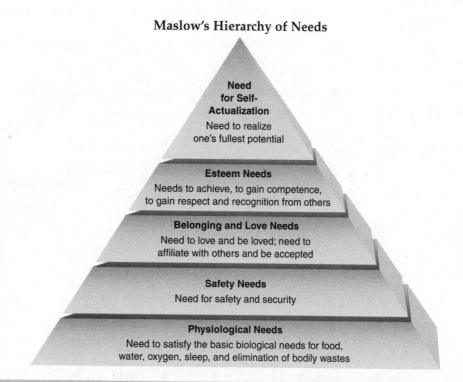

**Maslow's Hierarchy of Needs**

**Need for Self-Actualization**
Need to realize one's fullest potential

**Esteem Needs**
Needs to achieve, to gain competence, to gain respect and recognition from others

**Belonging and Love Needs**
Need to love and be loved; need to affiliate with others and be accepted

**Safety Needs**
Need for safety and security

**Physiological Needs**
Need to satisfy the basic biological needs for food, water, oxygen, sleep, and elimination of bodily wastes

| | |
|---|---|
| Module 9.2 The Primary Drives: Hunger and Thirst | 1. Thirst: We All Have Two Kinds |
| | 2. The Biological Basis of Hunger: Internal Hunger Cues |
| | 3. Other Factors Influencing Hunger: External Eating Cues |
| | 4. Understanding Variations in Body Weight: Why We Weigh What We Weigh |
| Module 9.3 Social Motives | 1. The Need for Achievement: The Drive to Excel |
| |     a. Atkinson's Theory of Achievement Motivation |
| |     b. Characteristics of Achievers |
| |     c. Developing Achievement Motivation |

| | |
|---|---|
| Module 9.4 The What and Why of Emotions | 1. Motivation and Emotion: What Is the Connection? |
| | 2. The Components of Emotions: The Physical, the Cognitive, and the Behavioural |
| | 3. Theories of Emotion: Which Comes First, the Thought or the Feeling?<br>a. The James-Lange Theory<br>b. The Cannon-Bard Theory<br>c. The Schachter-Singer theory<br>d. The Lazarus Cognitive-Appraisal Theory |
| Module 9.5 The Expression of Emotion | 1. The Range of Emotion: How Wide Is It? |
| | 2. The Development of Facial Expressions in Infants: Smiles and Frowns Come Naturally |
| | 3. Cultural Rules for Displaying Emotion |
| | 4. Emotion as a Form of Communication |
| World of Psychology | • Facial Expressions for the Basic Emotions—A Universal Language |

| Module 9.6 Experiencing Emotion | 1. The Facial-Feedback Hypothesis: Does the Face Cause the Feeling? |
| | 2. Emotion and Rational Thinking |
| | 3. Love: The Strongest Emotional Bond |
| World of Psychology | Gender Differences in the Experience of Emotion |
| Apply It! | Eating Disorders: The Tyranny of the Scale |

# Chapter Learning Objective Questions

Answer the following questions in the space provided and check your answers on the page numbers listed.

| | |
|---|---|
| 9.1 | What is the difference between intrinsic and extrinsic motivation? p. 282 |

| | |
|---|---|
| 9.2 | How do instinct theories explain motivation? p. 282 |

| | |
|---|---|
| 9.3 | What is the drive-reduction theory of motivation? p. 283 |

| | |
|---|---|
| 9.4 | How does arousal theory explain motivation? p. 284 |

| | |
|---|---|
| 9.5 | How does Maslow's hierarchy of needs account for human motivation? p. 286 |

| | |
|---|---|
| 9.6 | Under what kinds of conditions do the two types of thirst occur? p. 287 |

| | |
|---|---|
| 9.7 | What are the roles of the lateral hypothalamus and the ventro-medial hypothalamus in the regulation of eating behaviour? p. 287 |

| | |
|---|---|
| 9.8 | What are some of the body's hunger and satiety signals? p. 288 |

| | |
|---|---|
| 9.9 | What are some non-biological factors that influence what and how much we eat? p. 289 |

| | |
|---|---|
| 9.10 | What are some factors that account for variations in body weight? p. 290 |

9.11 How does set point affect body weight? p. 291

9.12 What is Henry Murray's contribution to the study of motivation? p. 292

9.13 What is the need for achievement? p. 292

9.14 What are some characteristics shared by people who are high in achievement motivation? p. 293

9.15 What are the three components of emotions? p. 294

9.16 According to the James-Lange theory, what sequence of events occurs when we experience an emotion? p. 295

9.17 What is the Cannon-Bard theory of emotion? p. 295

9.18 According to the Schachter-Singer theory, what two things must occur in order for us to experience an emotion? p. 295

9.19 According to Lazarus, what sequence of events occurs when an individual feels an emotion? p. 296

9.20 What are basic emotions? p. 297

| | |
|---|---|
| 9.21 How does the development of facial expressions of different emotions in infants suggest a biological basis for emotional expression? p. 297 | |
| 9.22 Why are emotions considered a form of communication? p. 299 | |
| 9.23 What is the facial-feedback hypothesis? p. 300 | |
| 9.24 How does Sternberg's triangular theory of love account for the different kinds of love? p. 303 | |
| | |
| | |
| | |
| | |
| | |
| | |

Learn to study more effectively and improve your memory with these tips and practical exercises.

## When Instructors Talk Too Fast

1. Read the material before class.

2. Review notes with classmates.

3. Leave large empty spaces in your notes.

4. Have a symbol that indicates to you that you have missed something.

5. Write down key points only and revise your notes right after class to add details.

6. Choose to focus on what you believe to be key information.

7. See the instructor after class and fill in what you missed.

8. Ask the instructor to slow down if you think that is appropriate.

## Staying With It

We have all experienced daydreaming or the voices in our mind that are busy judging and evaluating everything around us. These activities interfere without focusing on what we are trying to learn at the moment.

The following are ideas you can try the next time your mind takes time out:

1. Notice that your mind has wandered.

2. Don't fight it because the thought will just fight back.

3. Gently bring your mind back to the room.

4. Notice how your chair feels, what temperature the room is, and any smells in the room.

5. Practise noticing and letting go of your inner voices. It gets much easier with practice.

6. Your inner voices are helpful when you need to be creative or analytical. With practice you can quiet the voices when you are taking in new information and put the voices to good work when you are reviewing and organizing your notes.

# Improving Memory with Mnemonic Devices

Mnemonics are memory aids that have been developed to help us remember things. They include:

1. **Rhyme**—Organizing material so that it rhymes helps you to remember and ensures all of the material will be recalled in order.

2. **First-Letter Technique**—Arrange the first letters of each word into a list you need to remember. Form meaningful chunks out of the first letters, or use them to create a saying or phrase (e.g., Roy G. Biv for the colour spectrum, or Every Good Boy Deserves Fudge for the lines of the treble clef.

3. **Method of Loci**—If something needs to be recalled in a specific order, it may help to visualize the items in a location you are familiar with (e.g., your home).

4. **Keyword Method**—Imagining the new word you are trying to remember in an unusually vivid and bizarre manner may help you recall the information.

After studying the text and completing the Study Guide activities, answer these questions to determine if you need to review any areas before your exam.

1. Motivation is defined as a process that:
   a. initiates, directs, and sustains behaviour.
   b. changes behaviour as a result of prior experience.
   c. reflects physical and behavioural attempts to cope and adapt.
   d. is a relatively stable personality tendency.

2. Which of the following best describes extrinsic motivation?
   a. the desire to engage in an activity simply because it is enjoyable
   b. the desire to perform an act to gain a reward or to avoid an undesirable consequence
   c. the desire to perform an act that is part of instinctive behaviour
   d. working very hard to learn the principles of psychology because you find it interesting

3. An inborn, unlearned, fixed action pattern of behaviour that is characteristic of an entire species is referred to as:
   a. an emotion.
   b. an achievement motive.
   c. an instinct.
   d. an affiliation motive.

4. Drive-reduction theory assumes that various motives like hunger and thirst have in common the fact that they:
   a. are aroused by external stimuli.
   b. are unpleasant sensations we want to reduce or eliminate.
   c. cause us to behave in ways that increase our need level.
   d. are learned reactions.

5. The body's natural tendency to maintain a state of internal balance or equilibrium is referred to as:
   a. arousal.
   b. opponent process.
   c. homeostasis.
   d. instinct.

6. Which of the following theories suggests that the aim of motivation is to maintain an optimal level of arousal?
   a. attribution theory
   b. arousal theory
   c. drive-reduction theory
   d. instinct theory

7. According to the text, some researchers claim that emotional feelings are negative when people are:
   a. underaroused.
   b. overaroused.
   c. either underaroused or overaroused.
   d. at optimal arousal.

8. Which of the following suggests that performance on tasks is best when arousal levels are appropriate to the difficulty of the risk?
   a. instinctual theory of motivation
   b. James-Lange theory
   c. Maslow's hierarchy of needs
   d. the Yerkes-Dodson law

9. Which of the following conditions is not associated with prolonged sensory deprivation?
   a. inability to concentrate
   b. a satisfying, relaxed feeling
   c. hallucinations
   d. confusion

10. According to Maslow's hierarchy of needs, which of the following would need to be satisfied before a person would try to satisfy belonging and love needs?
    a. safety and self-actualization needs
    b. self-actualization and esteem needs
    c. physiological and safety needs
    d. physiological and esteem needs

11. One type of thirst develops from a loss of bodily fluid, which can be caused by all of the following except:
    a. perspiring.
    b. vomiting.
    c. excessive intake of alcohol.
    d. excessive intake of salt.

12. Which of the following is one of the body's satiety signals?
    a. high blood levels of glucose
    b. low blood levels of glucose
    c. high insulin levels
    d. stomach contractions

13. What hormone helps the body convert glucose to energy?
    a. the gastrointestinal hormone
    b. insulin
    c. CCK
    d. acetylcholine

14. The theory that suggests humans and other mammals are genetically programmed to maintain a certain amount of body weight is known as the:
    a. metabolic set theory.
    b. set-point theory.
    c. fat-cell theory.
    d. insulin utilization curve.

15. After trying many diets, losing and regaining weight repeatedly, a person can reach a point where the body gains weight quickly and loses it slowly. This phenomena of weight cycling is also called:
    a. set-point weight.
    b. fat-cell thermostat.
    c. yo-yo dieting.
    d. fat-cell theory.

16. How quickly your body burns calories to produce energy depends on your:
    a. set-point.
    b. metabolic rate.
    c. fat cells.
    d. food intake.

17. Increased exercise during dieting is important to counteract the body's tendency to:
    a. increase the fat in the fat cells.
    b. increase the number of fat cells.
    c. lower its metabolic rate.
    d. raise its metabolic rate.

18. The Thematic Apperception Text (TAT) involves showing subjects a series of ambiguous pictures and asking them to:
    a. remember them.
    b. write stories about them.
    c. reproduce them.
    d. correctly identify and label what each depicts.

19. Concerns with meeting standards of excellence and accomplishing difficult tasks refers to the:
    a. need for affiliation.
    b. need for achievement.
    c. need for power.
    d. need for apperception.

20. Individuals who are high in achievement motivation tend to:
    a. avoid opportunities for constructive feedback.
    b. prefer situations involving moderate levels of risk or difficulty.
    c. avoid opportunities that meet only moderate goals.
    d. prefer situations with very high task levels of risk or difficulty.

21. The three components of emotions are:
    a. stimulus, arousal, and release.
    b. arousal, loss of control, and regaining control.
    c. behaviour, physiological, and cognitive.
    d. motor, sensory, and cognitive.

22. The theory that emotional feelings result when we become aware of our physiological response to an emotion-provoking stimulus is the:
    a. Cannon-Bard theory.
    b. James-Lange theory.
    c. Schachter-Singer theory.
    d. facial feedback theory.

23. According to which of the following theories of emotion do the subjective reactions we label as fear and anxiety appear simultaneously with the physiological changes that accompany the emotion?
    a. Schachter-Singer theory
    b. Cannon-Bard theory
    c. James-Lange theory
    d. instinct theory

24. Some investigators have examined the facial expressions of subjects experiencing various basic emotions. When researchers compared the facial expressions of persons from different parts of the world, they found:
    a. little similarity in facial expressions across cultures.
    b. very similar facial expressions across cultures.
    c. extreme variations in most of the basic emotions.
    d. that few people are able to recognize these facial expressions.

25. The cultural rules that dictate how emotions should be expressed and where it is appropriate to express them are called:
    a. facial-feedback hypotheses.
    b. stimulus motives.
    c. display rules.
    d. gesture systems.

26. When subjects are instructed to exaggerate their facial expressions while viewing emotion-producing stimuli, it has been found that they:
    a. no longer report an emotional reaction to the stimuli.
    b. report a less intense emotional reaction to the stimuli.
    c. report an intensified emotional reaction to the stimuli.
    d. often report an emotional reaction that is opposite to the normally experienced emotion.

# Answers to Multiple Choice Questions

| Question Number | Answer | Learning Objective | Explanation for application questions |
|---|---|---|---|
| 1. | a. | 9.1 | |
| 2. | b. | 9.1 | Extrinsic motivation is rewards and punishments. |
| 3. | c. | 9.2 | |
| 4. | b. | 9.3 | |
| 5. | c. | 9.3 | |
| 6. | b. | 9.4 | |
| 7. | c. | 9.4 | |
| 8. | d. | 9.4 | |
| 9. | b. | 9.4 | |
| 10. | c. | 9.5 | |
| 11. | d. | 9.6 | One reason for thirst is loss of fluids due to perspiration, vomiting, or intake of alcohol. |
| 12. | a. | 9.8 | |
| 13. | b. | 9.8 | |
| 14. | b. | 9.11 | |
| 15. | c. | 9.12 | |
| 16. | b. | 9.12 | |
| 17. | c. | 9.12 | Exercise is able to counteract the body's natural tendency to decrease the metabolic rate when calories are reduced. |
| 18. | b. | 9.13 | |
| 19. | b. | 9.14 | |
| 20. | b. | 9.15 | |
| 21. | c. | 9.16 | |
| 22. | b. | 9.17 | James-Lange's theory states that emotional feelings result from awareness of our physiological state. |
| 23. | a. | 9.18 | |
| 24. | b. | 9.21 | |
| 25. | c. | 9.22 | |
| 26. | c. | 9.22 | |

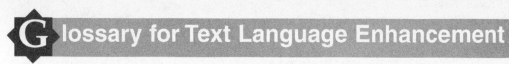

Students identified the following words from the text as needing more explanation. This page can be cut out, folded in half, and used as a bookmark for this chapter.

| term | definition |
| --- | --- |
| aspirations | what we hope to become |
| initiate | start |
| sustain | support |
| arousal | increased tension |
| sluggish | slow |
| chamber | small room |
| intricate | complex |
| invariant | not changing |
| dehydrated | took water out of |
| satiety | the feeling of having had more than one wants |
| obese | extremely overweight |
| distended | expanded |
| elevations | increases |
| mutated | changed |
| vigorously | with great effort |
| drawn to | attracted to |
| ambiguous | having no specific meaning; unclear |
| attain | gain, achieve |
| strive | try |
| peg | short stick |
| burglar | someone who steals things |
| frenzy | very nervous state |
| emerge | to come forth |
| stony-faced | show no emotion on your face |
| subtle | faint |
| swept away | overpowered by |
| eating binges | eating large amounts of food |
| purge | get rid of the food |
| gorge | to stuff oneself with food |
| triggers | starts |

# Thinking Critically

## Evaluation

In your view, which theory or combination of theories best explains motivation: drive-reduction theory, arousal theory, or Maslow's hierarchy of needs? Which theory do you find least convincing? Support your answers.

Using what you have learned about body weight and dieting, select any well-known weight-loss plan (for example, Weight Watchers, Jenny Craig, Slim-Fast) and evaluate it, explaining why it is or is not an effective way to lose weight and keep it off.

## Point/Counterpoint

Recent research suggests that individuals who work in the prevention of crime, such as police officers, airport security, and border officials, should be trained to read people's emotions since it is difficult to fake a true emotion. Prepare a convincing argument supporting each of the following positions:

a. Training security personnel to read facial expressions accurately should not be allowed.

b. Training security personnel to read facial expressions accurately should be allowed.

## Psychology in Your Life

Which level of Maslow's hierarchy (shown in Figure 9.2) provides the strongest motivation for your behaviour in general? Give specific examples to support your answer.

| | |
|---|---|
| motivation | drive-reduction theory |
| motives | drive |
| incentive | homeostasis |
| intrinsic motivation | arousal |
| extrinsic motivation | arousal theory |
| instinct | stimulus motives |
| instinct theory | Yerkes-Dodson law |

| | |
|---|---|
| A theory of motivation suggesting that a need creates an unpleasant state of arousal or tension called a drive, which impels an organism to engage in behaviour that will satisfy the need and reduce tension. | The process that initiates, directs, and sustains behaviour to satisfy physiological or psychological needs. |
| A state of tension or arousal brought about by an underlying need, which motivates one to engage in behaviour that will satisfy the need and reduce the tension. | Needs or desires that energize and direct behaviour toward a goal. |
| The tendency of the body to maintain a balanced internal state with regard to oxygen level, body temperature, blood sugar, water balance, and so forth to ensure physical survival. | An external stimulus that motivates behaviour (example: money, fame). |
| A state of alertness and mental and physical activation. | The desire to perform an act because it is satisfying or pleasurable in and of itself. |
| A theory suggesting that the aim of motivation is to maintain an optimal level of arousal. | The desire to perform an act to gain a reward or to avoid an undesirable consequence. |
| Motives that cause us to increase stimulation and that appear to be unlearned (examples: curiosity and the need to explore, manipulate objects, and play). | An inborn, unlearned, fixed pattern of behaviour that is characteristic of an entire species. |
| The principle that performance on tasks is best when the arousal level is appropriate—higher arousal for simple tasks, moderate arousal for tasks of moderate difficulty, and lower arousal for complex tasks. | The notion that human behaviour is motivated by certain innate tendencies, or instincts, shared by all individuals. |

| | |
|---|---|
| sensory deprivation | fat cells |
| hierarchy of needs | set point |
| self-actualization | social motives |
| primary drive | Thematic Apperception Test (TAT) |
| lateral hypothalamus | need for achievement |
| ventromedial hypothalamus | emotion |
| metabolic rate | James-Lange theory |

| | |
|---|---|
| Numbering 30 to 40 billion, cells that serve as storehouses for liquefied fat in the body; with weight loss, they decrease in size but not in number. | A condition in which sensory stimulation is reduced to a minimum or eliminated. |
| The weight the body normally maintains when one is trying neither to gain nor to lose weight (if weight falls below the normal level, appetite increases and metabolic rate decreases and vice versa.) | Maslow's theory of motivation, in which needs are arranged in order of urgency ranging from physical needs to security needs, belonging needs, esteem needs, and finally the need for self-actualization. |
| Motives acquired through experience and interaction with others. | The development of one's full potential; the highest need on Maslow's hierarchy. |
| A projective test consisting of drawings of ambiguous human situations, which the subject describes; thought to reveal inner feelings, conflicts, and motives. | A state of tension or arousal arising from a biological need; one not based on learning. |
| The need to accomplish something difficult and to perform at a high standard of excellence. | The part of the hypothalamus that supposedly acts as a feeding centre and, when activated, signals an animal to eat; when the LH is destroyed, the animal refuses to eat. |
| A feeling state involving physiological arousal, a cognitive appraisal of the situation arousing the state, and an outward expression of the state. | The part of the hypothalamus that presumably acts as a satiety centre and, when activated, signals an animal to stop eating; when the area is destroyed, the animal overeats, becoming obese. |
| The theory that emotional feelings result when we become aware of our physiological response to an emotion-provoking stimulus (for example, we are afraid because we tremble). | The rate at which the body burns calories to produce energy. |

| | |
|---|---|
| Cannon-Bard theory | consummate love |
| Schachter-Singer theory | Lazarus theory |
| obesity | |
| basic emotions | |
| display rules | |
| facial-feedback hypothesis | |
| triangular theory of love | |

| | |
|---|---|
| According to Sternberg's theory, the most complete form of love, consisting of three components—intimacy, passion, and commitment. | The theory that physiological arousal and the feeling of emotion occur simultaneously after an emotion-provoking stimulus is relayed to the thalamus and the cerebral cortex. |
| The theory that an emotion-provoking stimulus triggers a cognitive appraisal, which is followed by the emotion and physiological arousal. | A two-stage theory stating that for an emotion to occur, there must be (1) physiological arousal and (2) an explanation for the arousal. |
| | Excessive fatness; a term applied to men whose body fat exceeds 20% of their weight, and to women whose body fat exceeds 30% of their weight. |
| | Emotions that are found in all cultures, that are reflected in the same facial expressions across cultures, and that emerge in children according to their biological timetable (example: anger, disgust, happiness, sadness, distress). |
| | Cultural rules that dictate how emotions should be expressed, and when and where their expression is appropriate. |
| | The idea that the muscular movements involved in certain facial expressions trigger the corresponding emotions (for example, smiling makes us happy). |
| | Sternberg's theory that three components—intimacy, passion, and decision/commitment—singly and in various combinations produce seven different kinds of love. |

# 10

# SOCIAL PSYCHOLOGY

2. Romantic Attraction

3. Mate Selection: The Mating Game

| | |
|---|---|
| Module 10.3 Conformity, Obedience, and Compliance | 1. Conformity: Going Along with the Group<br><br>    • Asch's Experiment<br><br>2. Obedience: Following Orders<br><br>    • The Milgram Study<br><br>    • Variations of the Milgram Study<br><br>3. Compliance: Giving In to Requests<br><br>    • The Foot-in-the-Door Technique<br><br>    • The Door-in-the-Face Technique<br><br>    • The Low-Ball Technique<br><br>    • Wording of Requests<br><br>    • Increasing Guilt |
| Module 10.4 Group Influence | 1. The Effects of the Group on Individual Performance<br><br>    a. Social Facilitation: Performing in the Presence of Others |

Presence of Others (Audience effects, coaction effects) → Arousal heightened and dominant response enhanced → Performance is enhanced on tasks at which we are skilled and on simple tasks. / Performance suffers on tasks at which we are unskilled and on difficult tasks.

b.  Social Loafing: Not Pulling Our Weight in a Group Effort

2.  The Effects of the Group on Decision Making

a.  Group Polarization

b.  Group think

3.  Social Roles

- Zimbardo's Prison Study

| Module 10.5 Attitudes and Attitude Change | 1.  Attitudes: Cognitive, Emotional, and Behaviour Positions |
| | a.  The Relationship between Attitudes and Behaviour |

**The Three Components of an Attitude**

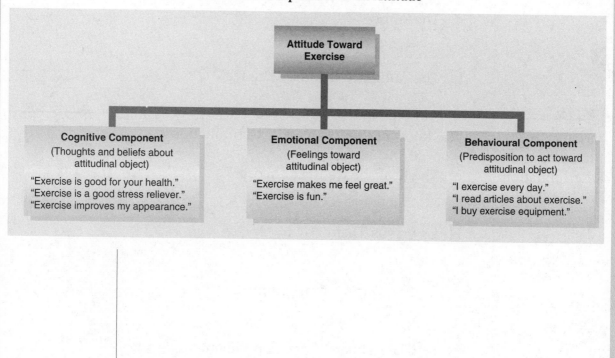

b.  Cognitive Dissonance: The Mental Pain of Inconsistency

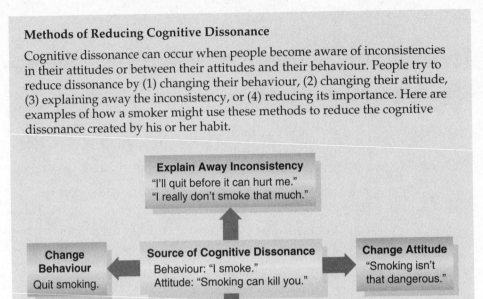

**Methods of Reducing Cognitive Dissonance**

Cognitive dissonance can occur when people become aware of inconsistencies in their attitudes or between their attitudes and their behaviour. People try to reduce dissonance by (1) changing their behaviour, (2) changing their attitude, (3) explaining away the inconsistency, or (4) reducing its importance. Here are examples of how a smoker might use these methods to reduce the cognitive dissonance created by his or her habit.

**Explain Away Inconsistency**
"I'll quit before it can hurt me."
"I really don't smoke that much."

**Change Behaviour**
Quit smoking.

**Source of Cognitive Dissonance**
Behaviour: "I smoke."
Attitude: "Smoking can kill you."

**Change Attitude**
"Smoking isn't that dangerous."

**Reduce Importance of Inconsistency**
"I have good genes. People in my family all live to a ripe old age."
"I exercise more and have a better diet than most people who smoke."
"No one in our family has ever had cancer."

2.  Persuasion: Trying to Change Attitudes

   a.  The Source

   b.  The Audience and the Message

---

Module 10.6
Prejudice and
Discrimination

1.  The Roots of Prejudice and Discrimination

   a.  The Realistic Conflict Theory

   b.  Us versus Them

      i.   In-group vs. Out-group

      ii.  The Robbers' Cave Experiment

    c. The Social Learning Theory

    d. Social Cognition

        i. Stereotypes

    e. Reverse Discrimination

2. Combating Prejudice and Discrimination

    a. Direct Contact: Bringing Diverse Groups Together

    b. Us versus Them: Extending the Boundaries of Narrowly Defined Social Groups

3. Prejudice: Is It Increasing or Decreasing?

---

**Module 10.7 Prosocial Behaviour: Behaviour That Benefits Others**

1. The Bystander Effect: The Greater the Number of Bystanders, the Less Likely They Are to Help

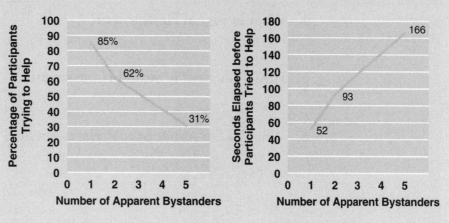

**The Bystander Effect**

In their intercom experiment, Darley and Latané showed that the more people a participant believed were present during an emergency, the longer it took that participant to respond and help a person in distress. (Data from Darley and Latané 1968a.)

|  | 2. People Who Help in Emergencies |
| --- | --- |
| Module 10.8 Aggression: Intentionally Harming Others | 1. Biological versus Social Factors in Aggression |
|  | 2. Aggression in Response to Frustration |
|  | Frustration–Aggression Hypothesis |
|  | Scapegoating |
|  | 3. Aggression in Response to Aversive Events: Pain, Heat, Noise, and More |
|  | 4. The Social Learning Theory of Aggression: Learning to Be Aggressive |
|  | • The Media and Aggression |
| Apply It! | Understanding Sexual Harassment |
|  | a. What Is Sexual Harassment? |
|  | b. How Prevalent is Sexual Harassment? |
|  | c. What To Do About Sexual Harassment |

# Chapter Learning Objective Questions

Answer the following questions in the space provided and check your answers on the page numbers listed.

| | |
|---|---|
| 10.1 Why are first impressions so important and enduring? p. 313 | |
| 10.2 What is the difference between a situational attribution and a dispositional attribution for a specific behaviour? p. 314 | |
| 10.3 How do the kinds of attributions we tend to make about ourselves differ from those we make about other people? p. 314 | |
| 10.4 Why is proximity an important factor in attraction? p. 315 | |
| 10.5 How important is physical attractiveness in attraction? p. 315 | |
| 10.6 Are people, as a rule, more attracted to those who are opposite or similar to them? p. 316 | |
| 10.7 What did Asch find in his famous experiment on conformity? p. 318 | |
| 10.8 What did Milgram find in his classic study of obedience? p. 319 | |
| 10.9 What are three techniques used to gain compliance? p. 321 | |
| 10.10 Under what conditions does social facilitation have either a positive or a negative effect on performance? p. 323 | |

10.11 What is social loafing, and what factors can lessen or eliminate it? p. 323

10.12 How are the initial attitudes of group members likely to affect group decision making? p. 324

10.13 What are the three components of an attitude? p. 326

10.14 What is cognitive dissonance, and how can it be resolved? p. 327

10.15 What are the four elements in persuasion? p. 327

10.16 What qualities make a source most persuasive? p. 328

10.17 What is the difference between prejudice and discrimination? p. 330

10.18 What is meant by the terms in-group and out-group? p. 330

10.19 How does prejudice develop, according to the social learning theory? p. 331

10.20 What are stereotypes? p. 331

| | |
|---|---|
| 10.21 What is reverse discrimination? p. 332 | |
| 10.22 What are several strategies for reducing prejudice and discrimination? p. 333 | |
| 10.23 What is the bystander effect and what factors have been suggested to explain why it occurs? p. 334 | |
| 10.24 What biological factors are thought to be related to aggression? p. 337 | |
| 10.25 What is the frustration–aggression hypothesis? p. 338 | |
| 10.26 What kinds of aversive events and unpleasant emotions have been related to aggression? p. 338 | |
| 10.27 According to social learning theory, what causes aggressive behaviour? p. 338 | |
| 10.28 What are the six responses to sexual harassment suggested in the Apply It! section? p. 340 | |
| | |
| | |

After studying the text and completing the Study Guide activities, answer these questions to determine if you need to review any areas before your exam.

1. Which of the following areas of psychology focuses on the influences other people have on our thoughts, feelings, and behaviours?
   a. personality psychology
   b. social psychology
   c. developmental psychology
   d. clinical psychology

2. Which of the following statements is true of first impressions?
   a. They act as filters for later information.
   b. They cannot be changed.
   c. They are usually correct.
   d. They are not particularly important.

3. When our expectations of another influence how the other person acts, the result is:
   a. a self-fulfilling prophecy.
   b. called the primary effect.
   c. referred to as the fundamental attribution error.
   d. a self-serving bias.

4. Attribution deals with the question of:
   a. why we and others act the way we do.
   b. how we can best achieve our goals.
   c. what the consequences of our actions will be.
   d. who our best choices for friends are.

5. The tendency of people to overemphasize dispositional causes and underemphasize situational causes when they explain the behaviour of others is called:
   a. the fundamental attributions.
   b. dispositional attributions.
   c. internal attributions.
   d. unbiased attributions.

6. Self-serving bias refers to our tendency to use:
   a. situational attributions for our behaviour.
   b. internal attributions for our behaviour.
   c. internal attributions for our successes and external attributions for our failures.
   d. internal attributions for our failures and external attributions for our successes.

7. The term that refers to the fact that interpersonal attraction is influenced by the physical closeness of other people to us:
   a. cognitive dissonance.
   b. ingratiation.
   c. proximity.
   d. priming.

8. Which of the following is best supported by research on interpersonal attraction?
   a. Familiarity breeds contempt.
   b. Absence makes the heart grow fonder.
   c. Opposites attract.
   d. Similarities attract.

9. When a person changes attitudes or behaviour to be consistent with the attitudes and behaviour of other people or with social norms, which of the following has occurred?
   a. conformity
   b. obedience
   c. deindividuation
   d. social facilitation

10. What is the term for a strategy used to gain first a favourable response to a small request, with the intent of making a person more likely to agree later to a larger request?
    a. planting-the-seed technique
    b. door-in-the-face technique
    c. foot-in-the-door technique
    d. that's-not-all-folks technique

11. The term social facilitation refers to:
    a. positive effects on one's performance due to the presence of others.
    b. negative effects on one's performance due to the presence of others.
    c. both positive and negative effects on one's performance due to the presence of others.
    d. negative effects on performance due to the absence of others.

12. Social loafing is most likely to occur when:
    a. individual output is monitored.
    b. individual output is evaluated.
    c. a task is challenging.
    d. individual output cannot be identified.

13. When group polarization occurs following group discussion, the group will decide to take a greater risk if they:
    a. were leaning in a cautious direction to begin with.
    b. were leaning in a risky direction to begin with.
    c. were leaning in different directions to begin with.
    d. regardless of the initial position of the group.

14. The three components of an attitude are:
    a. positive, negative, and neutral effect.
    b. the source, the message, and the medium.
    c. the cognitive, the emotional, and the behavioural.
    d. the opinion, the belief, and the knowledge.

15. Research on attitudes suggests that an attitude has all EXCEPT which of the following components?
    a. an emotional component
    b. a biochemical component
    c. a cognitive component
    d. a behavioural component

16. Which of the following would create the most cognitive dissonance?
    a. I bought a Toyota Corolla. I wish I had a Lexus.
    b. I like Italians. I don't like Italian food.
    c. I am an honest person. I cheated on the test.
    d. I should have gotten the job. I was not hired.

17. All of the following are components of persuasion except:
    a. the source.
    b. the framework.
    c. the message.
    d. the medium.

18. Prejudice is to _____ as discrimination is to _____.
    a. stereotypes; conflict
    b. attitudes; behaviours
    c. thought; competition
    d. in-group; out-group

19. According to the realistic conflict theory, prejudice develops because:
    a. realistic trait differences among ethnic groups are devalued rather than appreciated.
    b. human genes are programmed to compete with persons to whom we are not biologically related.
    c. of competition over scarce resources.
    d. individuals model the prejudice exhibited by family and friends.

20. Which of the following is an example of behaviour arising from us-versus-them social categories?
    a. helping a friend
    b. developing a sense of identity with your college because of its winning basketball team
    c. feeling insecure in an advanced psychology class you have chosen to take as an elective
    d. getting angry at the driver in the car in front of you

21. In the Robber's cave experiment, hostility and rivalry between two groups of boys was turned into cooperation by:
    a. having the two groups do pleasant activities together.
    b. having a crisis that requires both groups to work together.
    c. having an educational lecture on the value of cooperation.
    d. arranging for the two groups to have frequent contact with each other.

22. Recent research indicating that social cognition may play a role in the formation of prejudice and discrimination suggests that prejudice may spring from:
    a. our own natural thinking processes.
    b. in-group, out-group conflicts.
    c. competition among competing social groups.
    d. the realistic conflict theory.

23. The tendency to attribute generally positive or negative traits to a person as a result of observing one major positive or negative trait is called the:
a. halo effect.
b. exposure effect.
c. group think.
d. positive attribution theory.


24. According to social learning theory, attitudes of prejudice and hatred are learned by watching and mimicking:
a. parents.
b. teachers.
c. peers.
d. all of the above.

| Question Number | Answer | Learning Objective | Explanation for application questions |
|---|---|---|---|
| 1. | b. | 10.1 | |
| 2. | a. | 10.1 | |
| 3. | a. | 10.1 | |
| 4. | a. | 10.2 | |
| 5. | a. | 10.3 | |
| 6. | c. | 10.3 | |
| 7. | c. | 10.4 | |
| 8. | d. | 10.6 | |
| 9. | a. | 10.7 | |
| 10. | c. | 10.9 | |
| 11. | c. | 10.10 | |
| 12. | d. | 10.11 | |
| 13. | a. | 10.12 | |
| 14. | c. | 10.13 | |
| 15. | b. | 10.13 | |
| 16. | c. | 10.14 | |
| 17. | b. | 10.15 | |
| 18. | b. | 10.17 | |
| 19. | c. | 10.17 | |
| 20. | b. | 10.18 | |
| 21. | b. | 10.18 | |
| 22. | a. | 10.20 | |
| 23 | a. | 10.5 | |
| 24. | d. | 10.19 | Children copy the behaviour they see including prejudice and hatred toward different racial, ethnic, or cultural groups. |

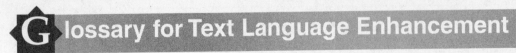
# Glossary for Text Language Enhancement

Students identified the following words from the text as needing more explanation. This page can be cut out, folded in half, and used as a bookmark for this chapter.

| term | definition |
|------|------------|
| composition | made up of |
| francophones | people who speak French |
| anglophones | people who speak English |
| vacuum | without outside influence |
| provocative | exciting or arousing |
| atrocious | extremely cruel |
| shallow | without much thought |
| overemphasize | magnify, focus on too much |
| underemphasize | focus on too little |
| exposure | to have experience with |
| socioeconomic | social class and financial level |
| conform | go along with |
| norm | what is typical |
| confederates | people helping the experimenter |
| unanimous | unified, going together |
| stunned | shocked, very surprised |
| atrocities | very terrible acts |
| strapped | held in by belts |
| hasten | hurry |
| flip | press up or down |
| frantic | in a panic |
| groan | sound made in pain |
| stutter | say extra letters when speaking |
| dig | push into |
| flesh | skin |
| defied | disobeyed |
| facilitation | help make something happen |
| polarization | having very different opinions |
| cohesiveness | the quality of being together |
| dissent | disagreement |
| invulnerable | cannot fail |
| hatched | created |
| indispensable | cannot do without |
| rounding up | gathering |
| deloused | treated for fleas |
| pool | a group to draw the participants from |
| sadistic | liking to cause pain |
| autonomous | independent, free to choose |
| inconsistency | always changing, not matched |

| term | definition |
|---|---|
| hatred | hate, extreme dislike |
| accusations | charges for wrong doing |
| berate | blame |
| vile | vulgar, filthy |
| insidious | in a dishonest manner |
| feminists | people who fight for the rights of women |

# Thinking Critically

## Evaluation

Many Canadians and Americans were surprised when the majority of the people in the Soviet Union rejoiced at the downfall of the communist system. Using what you have learned about attribution bias and conformity, try to explain why many Canadians mistakenly believed that the Soviet population preferred the communist system.

## Point/Counterpoint

Prepare a convincing argument supporting each of the following positions:

a. Aggression results largely from biological factors (nature).

b. Aggression is primarily learned (nurture).

## Psychology in Your Life

Review the factors influencing impression formation and attraction as discussed in this chapter. Prepare a dual list of behaviours indicating what you should and should not do if you wish to make a better impression on other people and increase their liking for you.

| | |
|---|---|
| social psychology | fundamental attribution error |
| | self-serving bias |
| | proximity |
| primacy effect | mere-exposure effect |
| attribution | halo effect |
| situational attribution | matching hypothesis |
| dispositional attribution | conformity |

| | |
|---|---|
| The tendency to overemphasize internal factors and underemphasize situational factors when explaining the behaviour of others. | The study of the way in which the actual, imagined, or implied presence of others influences the thoughts, the feelings, and the behaviour of individuals. |
| Our tendency to attribute our success to dispositional causes, and our failures to situational causes. | |
| Geographic closeness; a major factor in attraction. | |
| The tendency of people to develop a more positive evaluation of some person, object, or other stimulus with repeated exposure to it. | The likelihood that an overall impression of another to be influenced more by the first information that is received about that person than by information that comes later. |
| The tendency to attribute generally positive or negative traits to a person as a result of observing one major positive or negative trait. | An inference about the cause of our own or another's behaviour. |
| The notion that people tend to have spouses, lovers, or friends who are similar to themselves in social assets such as physical attractiveness. | Attribution of a behaviour to an external cause or factor operating in the situation; an external attribution. |
| Changing or adopting an attitude or behaviour to be consistent with the norms of a group or the expectations of others. | Attribution of one's own or another's behaviour to some internal cause such as a personal trait, motive, or attitude; an internal attribution. |

| | |
|---|---|
| norms | co-action effects |
| compliance | social loafing |
| foot-in-the-door technique | group polarization |
| door-in-the-face technique | groupthink |
| low-ball technique | roles |
| social facilitation | attitude |
| audience effects | cognitive dissonance |

| | |
|---|---|
| The impact on performance caused by the presence of others engaged in the same task. | The attitudes and standards of behaviour expected of members of a particular group. |
| The tendency to put forth less effort when working with others on a common task than when working alone. | Acting in accordance with the wishes, the suggestions, or the direct request of another person. |
| The tendency of members of a group, after group discussion, to shift toward a more extreme position in whatever direction they were leaning initially. | A strategy designed to secure a favourable response to a small request at first, with the aim of making the subject more likely to agree later to a larger request. |
| The tendency for members of a very cohesive group to feel pressure to maintain group solidarity and to reach agreement on an issue for which they fail adequately to weigh the evidence. | A strategy in which someone makes a large, unreasonable request with the expectation that the person will refuse but will then be more likely to respond favourably to a smaller request at a later time. |
| The behaviours considered to be appropriate for individuals occupying certain positions within the group. | A strategy to gain compliance by making a very attractive initial offer to get a person to agree to an action and then making the terms less favourable. |
| A relatively stable evaluation of a person, object, situation, or issue. | Any positive or negative effect on performance due to the presence of others; either as an audience or as co-actors. |
| The unpleasant state that can occur when people become aware of inconsistencies between their attitudes or between their attitudes and their behaviour. | The impact of passive spectators on performance. |

| | |
|---|---|
| persuasion | stereotypes |
| prejudice | reverse discrimination |
| discrimination | contact hypothesis |
| realistic conflict theory | bystander effect |
| in-group | diffusion of responsibility |
| out-group | prosocial behaviour |
| social cognition | altruism |

| | |
|---|---|
| Widely shared beliefs about the characteristic traits, attitudes, and behaviour of members of various social groups (racial, ethnic, religious) and including the assumption that *they* are usually all alike. | A deliberate attempt to influence the attitudes and/or behaviour of another. |
| Giving special treatment or higher evaluations to individuals from groups that have been the target of discrimination. | Negative attitudes toward others based on their gender, religion, race, or membership in a particular group. |
| The notion that prejudice can be reduced through increased contact among members of different social groups. | Behaviour, usually negative, directed toward others based on their gender, religion, race, or membership in a particular group. |
| The fact that as the number of bystanders at an emergency increases, the probability that the victim will receive help decreases, and help, if given, is likely to be delayed. | The notion that prejudices arise when social groups must compete for scarce resources and opportunities. |
| The feeling among bystanders at an emergency that the responsibility for helping is shared by the group, so each person feels less compelled to act than if he or she alone bore the total responsibility. | A social group with a strong sense of togetherness and from which others are excluded. |
| Behaviour that benefits others, such as helping, cooperation, and sympathy. | A social group specifically identified by the in-group as not belonging. |
| Behaviour aimed at helping another, requiring some self-sacrifice and not designed for personal gain. | Mental processes that people use to notice, interrupt, understand, remember, and apply information about the social world and that enable them to simplify, categorize, and order their world. |

| | |
|---|---|
| aggression | |
| frustration | |
| frustration-aggression hypothesis | |
| scapegoating | |
| actor-observer bias | |
| | |
| | |

|  | The intentional infliction of physical or psychological harm on another. |
|---|---|
|  | Interference with the attainment of a goal, or the blocking of an impulse. |
|  | The hypothesis that frustration produces aggression. |
|  | Displacing aggression onto minority groups or other innocent targets not responsible for the frustrating situation. |
|  | The tendency of observers to make dispositional attributions for the behaviours of others, but situational attributions for their own behaviour. |
|  |  |
|  |  |

# PERSONALITY THEORY AND ASSESSMENT

## 11

### CHAPTER OUTLINE

This outline provides a way to organize your notes from both the text and the lecture. It will also serve as a review for the exam.

| | |
|---|---|
| Module 11.1 Sigmund Freud and Psychoanalysis | 1. The Conscious, the Preconscious, and the Unconscious: Levels of Awareness |
| | 2. The Id, the Ego, and Superego: Warring Components of the Personality |

**Freud's Conception of the Personality**

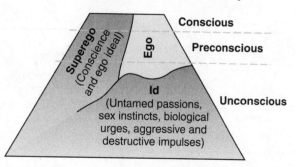

3. Defence Mechanisms: Protecting the Ego

4. The Psychosexual Stages of Development:
   Centred on the Erogenous Zones

   a. Oral Stage (Birth to 12 or 18 Months)

   b. The Anal Stage (12 or 18 Months to Age 3)

   c. The Phallic Stage (Ages Three to Five or Six)

   d. The Latency Period (Age Five or Six to Puberty)

   e. The Genital Stage (from Puberty On)

5. Freud's Explanation of Personality

6. Evaluating Freud's Contribution

---

Module 11.2
The
Neo-
Freudians

1. Carl Gustav Jung: Delving into the Collective Unconscious

**Jung's Conception of Personality**
Like Freud, Carl Jung saw three components in personality. The ego and the personal unconscious are unique to each individual. The collective unconscious is shared by all people and accounts for the similarity of myths and beliefs in diverse cultures.

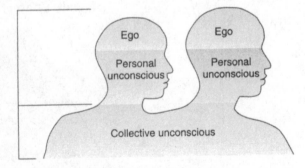

| | |
|---|---|
| | 2. Alfred Adler: Overcoming Inferiority |
| | 3. Karen Horney: Champion of Feminine Psychology |
| Module 11.3 Trait Theories | 1. Gordon Allport: Personality Traits in the Brain |
| | 2. Raymond Cattell's 16 Personality Factors |
| | 3. Hans Eysenck: Stressing Two Factors |
| | 4. The Five-Factor Theory of Personality: The Big Five |
| | 5. Evaluating the Trait Perspective |
| Module 11.4 Learning Theories and Personality | 1. The Behaviourist View of B. F. Skinner |
| | 2. The Social-Cognitive Theorists: Expanding the Behaviourist View |
| | |

| Module 11.5 Humanistic Personality Theories | 1. Abraham Maslow: The Self-Actualizing Person |
| | 2. Carl Rogers: The Fully Functioning Person |
| | 3. Evaluating the Humanistic Perspective |
| Module 11.6 Personality: Is It in the Genes? | 1. The Twin Study Method: Studying Identical and Fraternal Twins |
| Module 11.7 Personality Assessment | 1. Observation, Interviews, and Rating Scales |
| | 2. Personality Inventories: Taking Stock |
| | 3. Projective Tests: Projections from the Unconscious |
| | **An Inkblot similar to One on the Rorschach Inkblot Test** |
| Apply It! | 4. Is There Really a Sucker Born Every Minute? |

Answer the following questions in the space provided and check your answers on the page numbers listed.

| | | |
|---|---|---|
| 11.1 | To what two aspects of Freud's work does the term psychoanalysis apply? p. 348 | |
| 11.2 | What are the three levels of awareness in consciousness? p. 348 | |
| 11.3 | What are the roles of the id, the ego, and the superego? p. 349 | |
| 11.4 | What is a defence mechanism? p. 349 | |
| 11.5 | What are two ways in which repression operates? p. 349–350 | |
| 11.6 | What are some other defence mechanisms? p. 350 | |
| 11.7 | What are the psychosexual stages, and why did Freud consider them so important in personality development? p. 351 | |
| 11.8 | What is the Oedipus complex? p. 352 | |
| 11.9 | According to Freud, what are the two primary sources of influence on the personality? p. 353 | |
| 11.10 | According to Jung, what are the three components of personality? p. 355 | |

11.11 What did Adler consider to
be the driving force of the
personality? p. 355

11.12 Why is Horney considered
a pioneer in psychology?
p. 356

11.13 What are trait theories of
personality? p. 357

11.14 How did Allport differentiate
between cardinal and
central traits? p. 357

11.15 How did Cattell differentiate
between surface and source
traits? p. 358

11.16 What does Eysenck consider
to be the two most important
dimensions of personality?
p. 359

11.17 What are the Big Five personality dimensions in the five-
factor theory as described by
McCrae and Costa? p. 359

11.18 How did Skinner account
for what most people refer
to as personality? p. 361

11.19 What are the components
that make up Bandura's
concept of reciprocal determinism, and how do they
interact? p. 361

11.20 What is meant by the terms
internal and external locus of
control? p. 362

| | |
|---|---|
| 11.21 Who were the two pioneers in humanistic psychology, and how did they view human nature? p. 363 | |
| 11.22 What is self-actualization, and how did Maslow study it? p. 363 | |
| 11.23 According to Rogers, why don't all people become fully functioning persons? p. 363 | |
| 11.24 What has research in behavioural genetics revealed about the influence of the genes and environment on personality? p. 365 | |
| 11.25 What are the three major methods used in personality assessment? p. 366 | |
| 11.26 What is an inventory? What are the MMPI-2 and the Jackson Personality Inventory each designed to reveal? p. 366 | |
| 11.27 How do projective tests provide insight into personality, and what are several of the most commonly used? p. 368 | |
| | |
| | |
| | |

# Practice Multiple-Choice Test

After studying the text and completing the Study Guide activities, answer these questions to determine if you need to review any areas before your exam.

1. The definition of personality is based on observations that people:
   a. possess stable traits that uniquely distinguish them from others.
   b. are uniquely defined by traits that do not stabilize over time.
   c. differ only superficially from each other, and are basically alike.
   d. have stable traits that make them psychologically indistinguishable.

2. Sigmund Freud's theory is called:
   a. dynamic psychology.
   b. analytical psychology.
   c. psychoanalysis.
   d. psychic determinism.

3. According to Carl Rogers the main source for human emotional problems comes from people
   a. giving us a negative ego.
   b. setting up conditions of worth focus.
   c. being accepting and open with us too often.
   d. ignoring our behaviour.

4. The psychoanalytic system of the personality, which contains the life and death instincts and operates on the pleasure principle, is called the:
   a. ego
   b. id
   c. superego
   d. preconscious

5. The primary function of the ego is to:
   a. satisfy the desires of the id in a socially acceptable way.
   b. deny and overpower the id
   c. shift energy from the id to the superego
   d. promote behaviour that is unselfish and ethical

6. The superego is described as:
   a. an internalization of the moral teaching of our parents and society.
   b. a reality-oriented censor of behaviour.
   c. a manifestation of the instinct for survival of the species.
   d. a product of human evolution.

7. In the psychoanalytic view, what technique is used by the ego to protect against anxiety and to maintain self-esteem?
   a. free association
   b. fixation
   c. defence mechanism
   d. death instinct

8. Freud would say that the memories that have been removed from consciousness because they were too anxiety-provoking have been:
   a. repressed.
   b. expunged.
   c. repulsed.
   d. excised.

9. Ira denies his hatred for his brother Justin and claims that it is Justin who hates him. Ira may be using the defence mechanism called:
   a. rationalization.
   b. projection.
   c. sublimation.
   d. reaction formation.

10. Tony has just been informed that he is HIV positive. He refuses to believe it and insists that his test must have been confused with another's. Tony is probably using:
    a. reaction formation.
    b. sublimation.
    c. regression.
    d. denial.

11. Regression is defined as:
    a. attributing our own undesirable thoughts or behaviour to others.
    b. making excuses to justify our failures or mistakes.
    c. taking out our frustrations on a less threatening person or object.
    d. reverting to a behaviour that might have reduced anxiety at an earlier stage of development.

12. Freud theorized that the psychosexual stages occur in the order of:
    a. anal; oral; genital; phallic.
    b. oral; anal; phallic; genital.
    c. genital; anal; oral; phallic.
    d. anal; phallic; oral; genital.

13. According to Freud, the most important years in personality development were:
    a. from birth to 5 or 6.
    b. from 5 or 6 to puberty.
    c. adolescence.
    d. adulthood.

14. In Jung's theory, the inherited part of the personality, which stores the universal experiences of mankind is the:
    a. personal unconscious.
    b. impersonal unconscious.
    c. collective unconscious.
    d. universal unconscious.

15. People who see themselves as being able to perform competently and successfully in whatever they attempt, have what Bandura calls
    a. high self-regard
    b. a positive ego-picture
    c. reinforced behaviour
    d. high self-efficacy

16. _____ believed that we are driven by a need to overcome and compensate for inferiority feelings and strive for superiority and significance.
    a. Sigmund Freud
    b. Carl Jung
    c. Alfred Adler
    d. Karen Horney

17. Karen Horney argued that women really want the same opportunities and the rights and privileges afforded males in society. This view was meant to replace Freud's concept of:
    a. defence mechanisms.
    b. anxiety.
    c. superego.
    d. penis envy.

18. The particular ways we respond to the environment that remain fairly constant over time are called _____.
    a. norms
    b. egos
    c. traits
    d. clusters

19. According to Allport's theory, which of the following refers to a trait that is so strong a part of a person's life that he or she becomes identified with the trait?
    a. cardinal trait
    b. central trait
    c. primary trait
    d. ordinal trait

20. You tell your friend that you enjoy his company because he is fun-loving, intelligent, generous, and kind. According to Cattell, what type of traits are those?
    a. surface traits
    b. source traits
    c. primary traits
    d. secondary traits

21. Hans Eysenck's trait dimension of emotional stability versus instability is also known as:
    a. extroversion.
    b. introversion.
    c. psychoticism.
    d. neuroticism.

22. According to B. F. Skinner, which of the following ideas about personality was acceptable?
    a. Personality is a useful concept.
    b. We initiate and direct our own behaviour.
    c. Rewards and punishments shape our behaviour.
    d. Abnormal behaviour is primarily biological in origin.

| Question Number | Answer | Learning Objective | Explanation for application questions |
|---|---|---|---|
| 1. | a. | 11.1 | |
| 2. | c. | 11.1 | |
| 3. | b. | 11.23 | |
| 4. | b. | 11.3 | |
| 5. | a. | 11.3 | The ego attempts to find balance between the demands of the id and the strict rules of the superego. |
| 6. | a. | 11.3 | |
| 7. | c. | 11.4 | |
| 8. | a. | 11.5 | |
| 9. | b. | 11.6 | Projection is attributing one's own undesirable thoughts, impulses, traits, or behaviours to others. |
| 10. | d. | 11.6 | |
| 11. | d. | 11.6 | |
| 12. | b. | 11.7 | |
| 13. | a. | 11.9 | |
| 14. | c. | 11.10 | |
| 15. | d. | 11.19 | |
| 16. | c. | 11.11 | |
| 17. | d. | 11.12 | Karen Horney believed women do not envy men's penises, as Freud thought, but rather envy the privileges men enjoy. |
| 18. | c. | 11.13 | |
| 19. | a. | 11.13 | |
| 20. | a. | 11.17 | |
| 21. | d. | 11.17 | |
| 22. | c. | 11.18 | |

# Glossary for Text Language Enhancement

Students identified the following words from the text as needing more explanation. This page can be cut out, folded in half, and used as a bookmark for this chapter.

| term | definition |
| --- | --- |
| exempted | does not apply to them |
| equivalent | equal to |
| controversial | unsettled, debatable |
| heinous | terrible |
| impulse | stimulus, drive |
| minimize | make very small |
| exaggerate | make larger than it really is |
| inherited | inborn, born with |
| gratify | satisfy |
| tyrannical | mean, nasty |
| irrational | not reasonable |
| compatible | capable of getting along well together |
| lurk | hide |
| traumatic | terrible, very bad |
| rechannel | put in another area |
| puberty | body changes to adult |
| fixation | stuck in a spot |
| overindulgence | too much |
| gullibility | too trusting |
| sarcasm | hurtful words |
| stingy | selfish |
| stubborn | not willing to change |
| rigid | very firm |
| culminate | to end in |
| replicated | done again |
| gratify | satisfy |
| envy | jealousy |
| myths | stories, legends |
| tendency | way |
| consistent | always the same |
| essence | the basic, perhaps the most important, part of something |
| introspective | tending to look into one's own mind, emotions, or reactions |
| instability | unsteady, not stable |
| negligent | fail to do the right thing |
| vindictive | revengeful in spirit |
| boisterous | loud |
| easygoing | not easily angered |

| term | definition |
|------|-----------|
| reciprocal<br>severest | given or felt in return<br>most harsh |

# Thinking Critically

## Evaluation

In your opinion, which personality theory is the most accurate, reasonable, and realistic? Which is the least accurate, reasonable, and realistic? Support your answers.

## Point/Counterpoint

Are personality characteristics mostly learned? Or are they mostly transmitted through the genes? Using what you have learned in this chapter and other evidence you can gather, make a case for each position. Support your answers with research and expert opinion.

## Psychology in Your Life

Consider your own behaviour and personality attributes from the standpoint of each of the theories: psychoanalysis, trait theory, and the learning, humanistic, and genetic perspectives. Which theory or theories best explain your personality? Why?

| | |
|---|---|
| personality | ego |
| psychoanalysis | superego |
| conscious | defence mechanism |
| preconscious | repression |
| unconscious | projection |
| pleasure principle | denial |
| libido | rationalization |

| | |
|---|---|
| In Freudian theory, the rational, largely conscious system of personality, which operates according to the reality principle. | A person's unique and stable pattern of characteristics and behaviours. |
| The moral system of the personality, which consists of the conscience and the ego ideal. | Freud's term for his theory of personality and his therapy for treating psychological disorders. |
| An unconscious, irrational means used by the ego to defend against anxiety; involves self-deception and the distortion of reality. | The thoughts, feelings, sensations, and memories of which we are aware at any given moment. |
| The act of removing unpleasant memories from consciousness so that one is no longer aware of the pain event. | The thoughts, feelings, and memories that we are not consciously aware of at the moment but that may be brought to consciousness. |
| Attributing one's own undesirable thoughts, impulses, traits, or behaviours to others. | For Freud the primary motivating force of behaviour, containing repressed memories as well as instincts and wishes that have never been conscious. |
| Refusing to acknowledge consciously the existence of danger or a threatening condition. | The principle by which the id operates to seek pleasure, avoid pain, and obtain immediate gratification. |
| Supplying a logical, rational, socially acceptable reason rather than the real reason for an unacceptable thought or action. | Freud's name for the psychic or sexual energy that comes from the id and provides the energy for the entire personality. |

| | |
|---|---|
| regression | anal stage |
| reaction formation | phallic stage |
| displacement | Oedipus complex |
| sublimation | latency period |
| psychosexual stages | genital stage |
| fixation | personal unconscious |
| oral stage | collective unconscious |

| | |
|---|---|
| Freud's second psychosexual stage (ages 1 to 3 years), in which the child derives sensual pleasure mainly from expelling and withholding feces. | The act of reverting to a behaviour that might have reduced anxiety at an earlier stage of development. |
| Freud's third psychosexual stage (ages 3 to 5 or 6 years), during which sensual pleasure is derived mainly through touching the genitals, and the Oedipus complex arises. | Denying an unacceptable impulse, usually sexual or aggressive, by giving strong conscious expression to its opposite. |
| Occurring in the phallic stage, a conflict in which the child is sexually attracted to the opposite-sex parent and feels hostility toward the same-sex parent. | Substituting a less threatening object for the original object of an impulse. |
| The period following Freud's phallic stage (ages 5 or 6 to puberty), in which the sex instinct is largely repressed and temporarily sublimated in school, sports, and play activities. | Rechanneling sexual or aggressive energy into pursuits or accomplishments that society considers acceptable or admirable. |
| Freud's final psychosexual stage (from puberty on), in which for most people the focus of sexual energy gradually shifts to the opposite sex, culminating in the attainment of full adult sexuality. | A series of stages through which the sexual instinct develops; each stage is defined by an erogenous zone that becomes the centre of new pleasures and conflicts. |
| In Jung's theory, the layer of the unconscious containing all of the thoughts and experiences that are accessible to the conscious, as well as repressed memories and impulses. | Arrested development at a psychosexual stage occurring because of excessive gratification or frustration at that stage. |
| In Jung's theory, the most inaccessible layer of the unconscious, which contains the universal experience of humankind transmitted to each individual. | Freud's first psychosexual stage (birth to 1 or 1½ years), in which sensual pleasure is derived mainly through stimulation of the mouth. |

| | |
|---|---|
| archetype | surface traits |
| extraversion | source traits |
| introversion | five-factor theory |
| trait | reciprocal determinism |
| trait theories | self-efficacy |
| cardinal trait | locus of control |
| central trait | humanistic psychology |

| | |
|---|---|
| Cattell's name for observable qualities of personality, such as those used to describe a friend. | Existing in the collective unconscious, an inherited tendency to respond in particular ways to universal human situations. |
| Cattell's name for the traits that make up the most basic personality structure and cause behaviour. | The tendency to be outgoing, adaptable, and sociable. |
| A trait theory that attempts to explain personality using five broad dimensions, each of which is composed of a constellation of personality traits. | The tendency to focus inward; to be reflective, retiring, and nonsocial. |
| Bandura's concept that behaviour, personal/cognitive factors, and environment all influence and are influenced by each other. | A stable and consistent personal characteristic that is used to describe or explain personality. |
| A person's belief in his or her ability to perform competently in whatever is attempted. | Theories that attempt to explain personality and differences between people in terms of their personal characteristics. |
| How people account for what happens in their lives—those with an internal locus of control focus on being in control of their consequences; those with an external locus of control see things in the hands of fate. | Allport's name for a personal quality that is so strong a part of a person's personality that he or she may become identified with that trait. |
| An approach to psychology that stresses the uniquely human attributes and a positive view of human nature. | Allport's name for the type of trait you would use in writing a letter of recommendation. |

| | |
|---|---|
| self-actualization | MMPI-2 |
| conditions of worth | Jackson Personality Inventory |
| unconditional positive regard | projective test |
| behavioural genetics | Rorschach Inkblot Test |
| heritability | Thematic Apperception Test (TAT) |
| halo effect | id |
| inventory | |

| | |
|---|---|
| A revision of the most extensively researched and widely used personality test; used to screen and diagnose psychiatric problems and disorders. | Developing to one's fullest potential. |
| A highly regarded personality test used to assess the normal personality. | Conditions upon which the positive regard of others rests. |
| A personality test in which people respond to inkblots, drawings of ambiguous human situations, incomplete sentences, and the like, by projecting their own inner thoughts, feelings, fears, or conflicts onto the test materials. | Unqualified caring and nonjudgmental acceptance of another. |
| A projective test composed of ten inkblots to which a subject responds; used to reveal unconscious functioning and the presence of psychiatric disorders. | The field of research that investigates the relative effects of heredity and environment on behaviour and ability. |
| A projective test consisting of drawings of ambiguous human situations, which the subject describes; thought to reveal inner feelings, conflicts, and motives, which are projected onto the test materials. | An index of the degree to which a characteristic is estimated to be influenced by heredity. |
| The unconscious system of the personality, which contains the life and death instincts and operates on the pleasure principle. | The tendency of raters to be excessively influenced in their overall evaluation of a person by one or a few favourable or unfavourable traits. |
| | A paper-and-pencil test with questions about a person's thoughts, feelings, and behaviours, which measures several dimensions of personality. |

# 12

# HEALTH AND STRESS

## CHAPTER OUTLINE

This outline provides a way to organize your notes from both the text and the lecture. It will also serve as a review for the exam.

| Module 12.1 Theories of Stress | 1. Hans Selye and the General Adaptation Syndrome |
|---|---|

**The Biopsychosocial Model of Health and Wellness**
The biopsychosocial model focuses on health as well as illness and holds
that both are determined by a combination of biological, psychological, and
social factors. Most health psychologists endorse the biopsychosocial model.

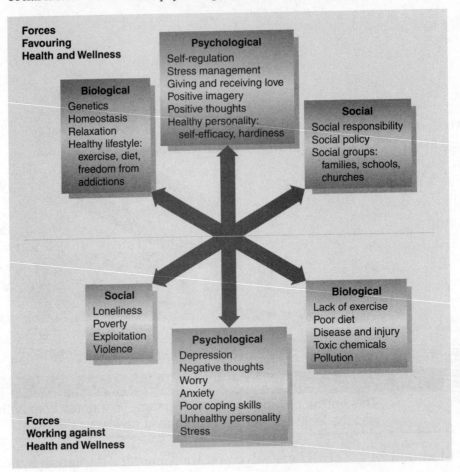

2. Richard Lazarus's Cognitive Theory of Stress

---

**Module 12.2
Sources of
Stress: The
Common and
the Extreme**

1. Everyday Sources of Stress

• Unpredictability and Lack of Control: Factors That Increase Stress

• Racism and Stress

2. Catastrophic Events and Chronic Intense Stress

3. Posttraumatic Stress Disorder

| | |
|---|---|
| Module 12.3 Coping with Stress | 1. Problem-Focused and Emotion-Focused Coping |
| Module 12.4 Evaluating Life Stress: Major Life Changes, Hassles, and Uplifts | 1. Holmes and Rahe's Social Readjustment Rating Scale: Adding Up the Stress Scores<br><br>2. The Hassles of Life: Little Things Stress a Lot |
| Module 12.5 Health and Disease | 1. Cancer: A Dreaded Disease<br><br>2. AIDS<br><br>3. Stress and the Immune System<br><br>4. Personal Factors Reducing the Impact of Stress and Illness |

| | |
|---|---|
| Module 12.6 Your Lifestyle and Your Health | 1. Smoking: Hazardous to Your Health |
| | 2. Alcohol: A Problem for Millions |
| | 3. Exercise: Keeping Fit Is Healthy |
| Apply It! | Managing Stress |
| | 1. Progressive Relaxation |
| | 2. Managing Mental Stress |
| | 3. Stress-Inoculation Training |
| | 4. Taking A Breather |
| | 5. Working Off Stress |

Answer the following questions in the space provided and check your answers on the page numbers listed.

| | |
|---|---|
| 12.1 | How do the biomedical model and biopsychosocial model differ in their approach to health and illness? p. 380 | |
| 12.2 | What is the general adaptation syndrome? p. 381 | |
| 12.3 | What are the roles of primary and secondary appraisal when people are confronted with a potentially stressful event? p. 383 | |
| 12.4 | How do approach–approach, avoidance–avoidance, and approach–avoidance conflicts differ? p. 384 | |
| 12.5 | How do the unpredictability of and lack of control over a stressor affect its impact? p. 384 | |
| 12.6 | How do people typically react to catastrophic events? p. 385 | |
| 12.7 | What is posttraumatic stress disorder? p. 385 | |
| 12.8 | What is the difference between problem-focused and emotion-focused coping? p. 387 | |
| 12.9 | What is the Social Readjustment Rating Scale designed to reveal? p. 389 | |
| 12.10 | What roles do hassles and uplifts play in the stress of life, according to Lazarus? p. 390 | |

12.11 What can cancer patients
do to help them cope with
having cancer? p. 393

12.12 What happens to a person
from the time of infection
with HIV to the development
of full-blown AIDS? p. 393

12.13 What are the effects of stress
and depression on the
immune system? p. 394

12.14 What three personal factors
are associated with health and
resistance to stress? p. 394

12.15 What constitutes an
unhealthy lifestyle, and how
serious a factor is lifestyle in
illness and disease? p. 396

12.16 Why is smoking considered
the single most preventable
cause of death? p. 396

12.17 What are some health risks of
alcohol consumption? p. 397

12.18 What are some benefits of
regular aerobic exercise?
p. 398

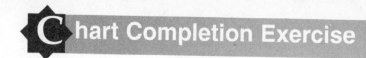

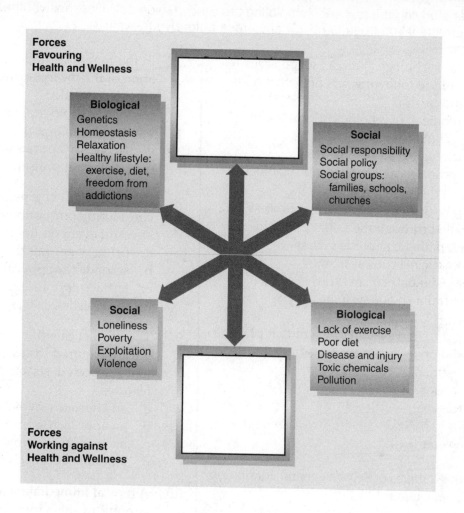

**Forces Favouring Health and Wellness**

**Biological**
Genetics
Homeostasis
Relaxation
Healthy lifestyle:
exercise, diet,
freedom from
addictions

**Social**
Social responsibility
Social policy
Social groups:
families, schools,
churches

**Social**
Loneliness
Poverty
Exploitation
Violence

**Biological**
Lack of exercise
Poor diet
Disease and injury
Toxic chemicals
Pollution

**Forces Working against Health and Wellness**

After studying the text and completing the Study Guide activities, answer these questions to determine if you need to review any areas before your exam.

1. The biopsychological model emphasizes which of the following sets of factors of illness and health?
   a. biological, psychological, and social
   b. psychological and genetic
   c. sociological and biomedical
   d. psychological, genetic, and sociological

2. The fight-or-flight response is a process controlled through the:
   a. sympathetic nervous system.
   b. somatic nervous system.
   c. parasympathetic nervous system.
   d. central nervous system.

3. A _____ is a stimuli or event that places a demand on an organism for adaptation or readjustment.
   a. stressor
   b. stress
   c. strain
   d. tension

4. The three stages of Selye's general adaptation syndrome are:
   a. perception, response, and recovery.
   b. perception, interpretation, and flight.
   c. alarm, resistance, and exhaustion.
   d. adaptation, modification, and adoption.

5. During what stage of the general adaptation syndrome is susceptibility to illness increased?
   a. alarm
   b. terminal
   c. resistance
   d. exhaustion

6. Some psychologists believe that Selye failed to consider the:
   a. physiological component of stress.
   b. psychological component of stress.
   c. health consequences of stress.
   d. impact of stress on animals.

7. In the cognitive model of stress, the evaluation of the meaning and significance of a situation is called:
   a. the psychological stressor.
   b. the physiological stressor.
   c. secondary appraisal.
   d. primary appraisal.

8. Evaluating our coping resources and considering our options in dealing with a stressful event occurs during:
   a. primary appraisal.
   b. secondary appraisal.
   c. tertiary appraisal.
   d. the resistance stage.

9. The conflict called _____ occurs whenever we are required to select an alternative that has both desirable and undesirable features.
   a. an approach–avoidance conflict
   b. an approach–approach conflict
   c. an avoidance–avoidance conflict
   d. a double approach–avoidance conflict

10. A typical immediate reaction to a catastrophic event is for a person to be:
    a. in a state of panic.
    b. highly emotional.
    c. dazed, stunned, and emotionally numb.
    d. composed enough to help others.

11. People suffering from posttraumatic stress disorder may experience all of the following EXCEPT:
    a. They startle easily.
    b. They are anxious.
    c. They have nightmares and flashbacks.
    d. Their symptoms are not readily apparent.

12. Problem-focused coping strategies are most useful in situations that are:
    a. moderately stressful.
    b. extremely stressful.
    c. unchangeable.
    d. changeable.

13. An example of emotion-focused coping is
    _____.
    a. studying or working harder
    b. humour
    c. talking the problem over with an expert
    d. writing a letter to your MP

14. Well-functioning people use:
    a. mostly problem-focused coping.
    b. mostly emotion-focused coping.
    c. a combination of problem-focused and emotion-focused coping.
    d. a minimum of problem-focused and emotion-focused coping.

15. When you are experiencing a lot of stress you can reduce the impact of the stress by helping others. How does this work?
    a. those you help will take your stress away
    b. it makes you feel less like a victim and more like a contributor
    c. you cannot think of two things at once, helping and your distress
    d. it will not help, your stress is unchangeable

16. According to Holmes and Rahe, persons who experience a number of major life changes over the course of a year are likely to have what kind of experience in the next two years?
    a. change jobs more frequently than usual
    b. have a high probability of getting a divorce
    c. have a high probability of committing a crime
    d. experience more health problems than usual

17. According to Lazarus, what usually causes the average person the most stress?
    a. major life changes
    b. catastrophic events
    c. hassles
    d. approach-avoidance conflicts

18. The term _____ refers to the positive experiences in life that can neutralize the effects of many of the hassles.
    a. highs
    b. uplifts
    c. peak experiences
    d. destressors

19. The research on coping with the distress of cancer has found that _____ reduces the distress.
    a. a pessimistic outlook
    b. surrendering to the disuse
    c. social support
    d. a serious attitude

20. What is the relationship between stress and the immune system?
    a. stress helps the immune system become tough
    b. lower stress levels weaken the immune system
    c. the immune system prevents stress responses
    d. high levels of stress are related to lower immune activity

21. According to Parrott (1993) why do most people smoke?
    a. it serves as a coping mechanism for regulating moods
    b. they enjoy the activity
    c. they are simple copying other people's behaviour
    d. for status and image enhancement

22. Research on environmental influences leading to alcohol abuse or alcoholism suggests:
    a. genetics play the major role in causing the problem.
    b. all alcoholics can learn to drink socially.
    c. sons of alcoholics are less likely to drink if they are adopted into another family than sons of non-alcoholics.
    d. behavioural, social, and cultural factors play a role in alcoholism.

# Answers to Multiple-Choice Questions

| Question Number | Answer | Learning Objective | Explanation for application questions |
|---|---|---|---|
| 1. | a. | 12.1 | |
| 2. | a. | 12.2 | |
| 3. | a. | 12.2 | |
| 4. | c. | 12.2 | |
| 5. | d. | 12.2 | |
| 6. | b. | 12.2 | |
| 7. | d. | 12.3 | |
| 8. | b. | 12.3 | |
| 9. | a. | 12.4 | |
| 10. | c. | 12.6 | |
| 11. | d. | 12.7 | |
| 12. | d. | 12.8 | |
| 13. | b. | 12.8 | |
| 14. | c. | 12.8 | |
| 15. | b. | 12.8 | |
| 16. | d. | 12.9 | |
| 17. | c. | 12.10 | |
| 18. | b. | 12.10 | |
| 19. | c. | 12.11 | |
| 20. | d. | 12.13 | |
| 21. | a. | 12.16 | |
| 22. | d. | 12.17 | |

# Glossary for Text Language Enhancement

Students identified the following words from the text as needing more explanation. This page can be cut out, folded in half, and used as a bookmark for this chapter.

| term | definition |
|---|---|
| debilitating | weakening |
| degenerative disease | an illness that causes a continued decline in health |
| on the verge | just about to do something |
| brooding | dwelling on |
| exhilaration | excitement |
| depleted | exhausted |
| appraisal | analysis |
| orthodox | agreeing with the established beliefs |
| catastrophic | horrible |
| aimlessly | without purpose |
| disintegration | separate into parts |
| cope | deal with |
| myriad | a large number of things |
| scourge | inflicts severe suffering |
| succumb | open to |
| craving | strong desire (want) |
| total abstinence | not using any alcohol at all |
| strenuous | difficult |

# Thinking Critically

## Evaluation

Can people always cure themselves of illnesses? What are the limits to what people can do to help themselves?

## Point/Counterpoint

Prepare two arguments, one supporting the position that alcoholism is a genetically inherited disease, and the other supporting the position that alcoholism is not a medical disease but results from learning.

## Psychology in Your Life

Choose several stress-producing incidents from your own life and explain what problem-focused and emotion-focused coping strategies you used. From the knowledge you have gained in this chapter, list other coping strategies that might have been more effective.

| | |
|---|---|
| biomedical | resistance stage |
| biopsychosocial model | exhaustion stage |
| health psychology | primary appraisal |
| stress | secondary appraisal |
| stressor | approach-approach conflict |
| general adaptation syndrome (GAS) | avoidance-avoidance conflict |
| alarm stage | approach-avoidance conflict |

| | |
|---|---|
| The second stage of the general adaptation syndrome, when there are intense physiological efforts to resist or adapt to the stressor. | A perspective that focuses on illness rather than health, explaining illness in terms of biological factors without regard to psychological and social factors. |
| The final stage of the general adaptation syndrome, occurring if the organism fails in its efforts to resist the stressor. | A perspective that focuses on health as well as illness and holds that both are determined by a combination of biological, psychological, and social factors. |
| Evaluating the significance of a potentially stressful event according to how it will affect one's well-being—whether it is perceived as irrelevant or as involving harm or loss, threat, or challenge. | The field concerned with the psychological factors that contribute to health, illness, and response to illness. |
| Evaluating one's coping resources and deciding how to deal with a stressful event. | The physiological and psychological response to a condition that threatens or challenges a person and requires some form of adaptation or adjustment. |
| A conflict arising from having to choose between desirable alternatives. | Any event capable of producing physical or emotional stress. |
| A conflict arising from having to choose between two undesirable alternatives. | The predictable sequence of reactions (alarm, resistance, and exhaustion stages) that organisms show in response to stressors. |
| A conflict arising when the same choice has both desirable and undesirable features. | The first stage of the general adaptation syndrome, when there is emotional arousal and the defensive forces of the body are prepared for fight or flight. |

| | |
|---|---|
| posttraumatic stress disorder (PTSD) | |
| coping | emotion-focused coping |
| problem-focused coping | psychoneuro-immunology |
| Social Readjustment Rating Scale (SRRS) | hardiness |
| hassles | social support |
| uplifts | controlled drinking |
| | aerobic exercise |

| | A prolonged and severe stress reaction to a traumatic event, characterized by anxiety, psychic numbing, withdrawal from others, and feeling of reliving the experience. |
|---|---|
| A response aimed at reducing the emotional impact of the stressor. | Efforts through action and thought to deal with demands that are perceived as taxing or overwhelming. |
| A field in which psychologists, biologists, and medical researchers study the effects of psychological factors on the immune system. | A response aimed at reducing, modifying, or eliminating a source of stress. |
| A combination of three psychological qualities shared by people who can undergo high levels of stress yet remain healthy: a sense of control, commitment to goals, and ability to view change as a challenge. | A stress scale developed by Holmes and Rahe, which ranks 43 different life events from most to least stressful and assigns a point value to each. |
| Tangible support, information, advice, and/or emotional support provided in time of need by family, friends, and others; the feeling that we are loved, valued, and cared for. | Little stressors that include the irritating demands and troubled relationships that can occur daily and that, according to Lazarus, cause more stress than do major life changes. |
| A behavioural approach to the treatment of alcoholism, designed to teach the skills necessary so that alcoholics can drink socially without losing control. | The positive experiences in life, which can neutralize the effects of many of the hassles. |
| Exercise that uses the large muscle groups in continuous, repetitive action and requires increased oxygen intake and increased breathing and heart rate. | |

# 13

# PSYCHOLOGICAL DISORDERS

|  | 2. Defining and Classifying Psychological Disorders |
|---|---|
| Module 13.2<br>Anxiety<br>Disorders:<br>When Anxiety<br>Is Extreme | 1. Generalized Anxiety Disorder<br><br>2. Panic Disorder<br><br>3. Phobias: Persistent, Irrational Fears<br><br>4. Obsessive Compulsive Disorder |
| Module 13.3<br>Somatoform<br>and<br>Dissociative<br>Disorders | 1. Somatoform Disorders: Physical Symptoms with Psychological Causes<br><br>   a. Hypochondriasis<br><br>   b. Conversion Disorder: When Thoughts and Fears Can Paralyze<br><br>2. Dissociative Disorders: Mental Escapes<br><br>   a. Dissociative Amnesia<br><br>   b. Dissociative Fugue |

|  |  |
|---|---|
|  | c. Dissociative Identity Disorder |
| Module 13.4<br>Schizophrenia | 1. The Symptoms of Schizophrenia |
|  |   a. Positive Symptoms |
|  |     • Hallucinations |
|  |     • Delusions |
|  |     • Disturbances in the Form of Thought or Speech |
|  |     • Grossly Disorganized Behaviour |
|  |     • Inappropriate Affect |
|  |   b. Negative Symptoms |
|  |     • Social withdrawal, apathy, loss of motivation, lack of goal-directed activity, limited speech, slow movements, poor hygiene and grooming, poor problem-solving abilities, and a distorted sense of time |
|  |   c. Brain Abnormalities in Some Schizophrenics |
|  | 2. Types of Schizophrenia |
|  |   a. Catatonic |
|  |   b. Disorganized |
|  |   c. Paranoid |
|  |   d. Undifferentiated |

3. The Causes of Schizophrenia

   a. Genetic Inheritance

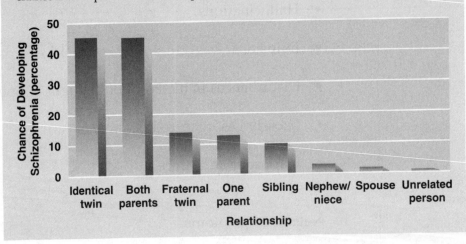

**Genetic Similarity and Probability of Developing Schizophrenia**

Research strongly indicates a genetic factor operating in many cases of schizophrenia. Identical twins have identical genes, and if one twin develops schizophrenia, the other twin has a 46 percent chance of developing it also. In fraternal twins the chance is only 14 percent. A person with one schizophrenic parent has a 13 percent chance of developing schizophrenia, but a 46 percent chance if both parents are schizophrenic. (Data from Nicol and Gottesman 1983.)

   b. Excessive Dopamine Activity

4. Gender and Schizophrenia

---

**Module 13.5 Mood Disorders**

1. Depressive Disorders and Bipolar Disorder: Emotional Highs, and Lows

   a. Major Depressive Disorder

   b. Seasonal Depression

   c. Bipolar Disorder

2. Causes of Major Depressive Disorder and Bipolar Disorder

    a. The Biological Perspective

    b. The Cognitive Perspective

| Module 13.6 Other Psychological Disorders | 1. Personality Disorders: Troublesome Behaviour Patterns<br><br>    • Antisocial Personality Disorder<br><br><br><br>2. Sexual and Gender Identity Disorders |
|---|---|
| Apply It! | Depression: Bad Thoughts, Bad Feelings |

Answer the following questions in the space provided and check your answers on the page numbers listed.

13.1 What criteria might be used to differentiate normal from abnormal behaviour? p. 408

13.2 What are five current perspectives that attempt to explain the causes of psychological disorders? p. 409

13.3 What is the DSM-IV-TR? p. 410

13.4 When is anxiety healthy, and when is it unhealthy? p. 412

13.5 What are the symptoms of panic disorder? p. 413

13.6 What are the characteristics of the three categories of phobias? p. 413

13.7 What do psychologists believe are some probable causes of phobias? p. 415

13.8 What is obsessive-compulsive disorder? p. 415

13.9 What are two somatoform disorders, and what symptoms do they share? p. 417

13.10 What is dissociative amnesia? p. 418

13.11 What is dissociative figure?
p. 418

13.12 What are some of the identifying symptoms of dissociative identity disorder? p. 420

13.13 What are some of the major
positive symptoms of schizophrenia? p. 420

13.14 What are some of the major
negative symptoms of
schizophrenia? p. 420

13.15 What are the four subtypes of
schizophrenia? p. 421

13.16 What are some suggested
causes of schizophrenia?
p. 422

13.17 What are the symptoms of
major depressive disorder?
p. 423

13.18 What are the extremes of
mood suffered in bipolar
disorder? p. 426

13.19 What are some suggested
causes of major depressive
disorder and bipolar disorder?
p. 426

13.20 What are the main attributes
of personality disorders?
p. 427

13.21 What are the sexual and
gender identity disorders?
p. 430

# Practice Multiple-Choice Test

After studying the text and completing the Study Guide activities, answer these questions to determine if you need to review any areas before your exam.

1. All of the following are true about the distinction between normal and abnormal behaviour EXCEPT:
   a. A person might be considered normal in one culture and abnormal in another.
   b. Not all people whose behaviour is abnormal experience personal distress.
   c. The most widely used criterion for committing people to an institution is whether they are a danger to themselves or others.
   d. It is relatively easy to differentiate normal behaviour from abnormal behaviour.

2. A psychologist is convinced that abnormal behaviours arise from structural abnormalities and chemical imbalances in the brain. His view of abnormal behaviour is most consistent with the:
   a. psychodynamic perspective.
   b. humanistic perspective.
   c. cognitive perspective.
   d. biological perspective.

3. Which perspective suggests that unconscious sexual or aggressive conflicts in early childhood experiences are the cause of abnormal behaviour?
   a. cognitive perspective
   b. humanistic perspective
   c. psychodynamic perspective
   d. biological perspective

4. Which is a suggested cause of abnormal behaviour from the cognitive perspective?
   a. faulty learning
   b. early childhood experiences
   c. unconscious, unresolved conflicts
   d. faulty thinking

5. Which of the following perspectives suggests that psychological disorders arise from the blocking of a person's natural tendency toward self-actualization?
   a. the humanistic perspective
   b. the learning perspective
   c. the biological perspective
   d. the cognitive perspective

6. The DSM-IV-TR is a manual published by the American Psychiatric Association that is used to:
   a. diagnose mental disorders.
   b. explain the causes of mental disorders.
   c. outline treatments for various mental disorders.
   d. assess the effectiveness of treatment programs.

7. The diagnosis of generalized anxiety disorder applies to people who:
   a. are feeling bad about their anxiety.
   b. are experiencing an unusual change in their lives that is causing anxiety.
   c. are having irrational thoughts and suicidal tendencies.
   d. are experiencing excessive anxiety that they cannot control.

8. The disorder characterized by recurrent and unpredictable attacks of anxiety, panic, or terror is known as:
   a. panic disorder.
   b. obsessive-compulsive disorder.
   c. generalized anxiety disorder.
   d. phobia.

9. A persistent, irrational fear of some object, situation, or activity that a person feels compelled to avoid is called:
   a. an avoidance response.
   b. a phobia.
   c. a panic attack.
   d. an obsession.

10. A persistent recurring involuntary thought, image, or impulse that invades consciousness and causes great distress is called:
    a. a hallucination.
    c. a delusion.
    b. an obsession.
    d. a compulsion.

11. A behaviour that a person feels driven to perform is called:
    a. a hallucination.
    b. an obsession.
    c. a delusion.
    d. a compulsion.

12. People who are preoccupied with their health and convinced they have some serious disorder despite reassurances from medical doctors to the contrary are usually suffering from:
    a. conversion disorder.
    b. psychogenic illness.
    c. psychosomatic neurosis.
    d. hypochondriasis.

13. Becky saw her brother get killed at a restaurant. She has not been able to see since that night even though doctors say there is nothing wrong with her eyes. Becky is probably suffering from:
    a. conversion disorder.
    b. an anxiety disorder.
    c. a phobia.
    d. a dissociative disorder.

14. What is the disorder in which two or more distinct personalities exist in a person, each personality taking over at different times?
    a. dissociative amnesia
    b. split personality
    c. dissociative identity disorder
    d. schizophrenia

15. A(n) _____ is occurring when a person sees, hears, smells, or tastes something when there is nothing causing the sensation.
    a. a hallucination
    b. a delusion
    c. an obsession
    d. a compulsion

16. Delusions are _____ while hallucinations are _____.
    a. irrational thoughts; unusual sensations
    b. unusual sensations; irrational thoughts
    c. false beliefs; imaginary sensations
    d. imaginary sensations; false beliefs

17. Someone with a diagnosis of _____ believes people are after him and trying to hurt him, even though this is not true.
    a. catatonic schizophrenia
    b. disorganized schizophrenia
    c. undifferentiated schizophrenia
    d. paranoid schizophrenia

18. Drugs effective in treating schizophrenia:
    a. block the action of norepinephrine in the brain.
    b. reduce blood flow in the brain.
    c. block the action of dopamine in the brain.
    d. increase melatonin levels in the brain.

19. The most frequently occurring major psychological disorder is:
    a. phobias.
    b. schizophrenia.
    c. bipolar disorder.
    d. depression.

20. What is the term for a period of extreme elation, euphoria, and hyperactivity, which is often accompanied by delusions of grandeur?
    a. seasonal euphoric episode
    b. delusional euphoric episode
    c. manic episode
    d. hyperinflationary state

21. Low levels of neurotransmitters such as norepinephrine and serotonin are associated with _____; high levels of these same neurotransmitters are associated with _____.
    a. mania; schizophrenia
    b. depression; schizophrenia
    c. depression; mania
    d. mania; depression

22. A disorder in which a bizarre practice is necessary for sexual gratification is called a(n):
    a. sexual dysfunction.
    b. impaired sexual performance.
    c. paranormia.
    d. inorgasmia.

| Question Number | Answer | Learning Objective | Explanation for application questions |
|---|---|---|---|
| 1. | d. | 13.1 | |
| 2. | d. | 13.2 | |
| 3. | c. | 13.2 | |
| 4. | d. | 13.2 | |
| 5. | a. | 13.2 | |
| 6. | a. | 13.3 | |
| 7. | d. | 13.4 | |
| 8. | a. | 13.5 | |
| 9. | b. | 13.6 | |
| 10. | b. | 13.8 | |
| 11. | d. | 13.8 | |
| 12. | d. | 13.9 | |
| 13. | a. | 13.9 | |
| 14. | c. | 13.12 | |
| 15. | a. | 13.13 | |
| 16. | c. | 13.13 | |
| 17. | d. | 13.15 | |
| 18. | c. | 13.13 | |
| 19. | d. | 13.17 | |
| 20. | c. | 13.18 | |
| 21. | c. | 13.19 | |
| 22. | a. | 13.20 | |

# Glossary for Text Language Enhancement

Students identified the following words from the text as needing more explanation.
This page can be cut out, folded in half, and used as a bookmark for this chapter.

| term | definition |
|---|---|
| advocacy | acting on behalf of others, to help |
| clear-cut | obvious |
| obsolete | gone out of use |
| vague | not specific |
| prompts | helps |
| unduly | unnecessarily |
| sheds | gives |
| clumsy | to fall easily |
| catch-all | contains many different types |
| raw | sore |
| stabbing | putting a knife into |
| intolerable | too painful to deal with |
| alter- | other personality |
| forth | forward |
| menacing | threatening |
| dishevelled | unclean; not orderly |
| agitation | becoming forceful, violent |
| stupor | a state in which the mind and senses are dulled |
| grimaces | twisting of the face |
| incoherent | not making sense |
| elation | extreme happiness |
| despair | extreme unhappiness |
| disproportionately | in a manner that is not equal |
| recurrence | happening again |
| euphoria | feeling very good |
| wound up | full of energy |
| spending sprees | spending a lot of money |
| enraged | feeling extreme anger |
| remorse | being sorry for something |
| gender | male or female |

# Thinking Critically

## Evaluation

Some psychological disorders are more common in women (depression, agoraphobia, and specific phobia), and some are more common in men (antisocial personality disorder and substance-related disorders). Give some possible reasons why such gender differences exist in these disorders. Support your answer.

## Point/Counterpoint

There is continuing controversy over whether specific psychological disorders are chiefly biological in origin (nature) or result primarily from learning and experience (nurture). Select any two disorders from this chapter and prepare arguments for both nature and nurture for both disorders.

## Psychology in Your Life

Formulate a specific plan for your own life that will help you recognize and avoid the five cognitive traps that contribute to unhealthy thinking. You might enlist the help of a friend to monitor your negative statements.

| | |
|---|---|
| DSM-IV-TR | panic disorder |
| neurosis | phobia |
| psychosis | agoraphobia |
| undifferentiated schizophrenia | social phobia |
| anxiety | specific phobia |
| generalized anxiety disorder | obsessive compulsive disorder |
| panic attack | obsession |

| | |
|---|---|
| An anxiety disorder in which a person experiences recurrent unpredictable attacks or over-whelming anxiety, fear, or terror. | The *Diagnostic and Statistical Manual of Mental Disorders* (fourth edition revised); describes about 290 mental disorders and the symptoms that must be present for diagnosing each disorder. |
| A persistent, irrational fear of an object, situation, or activity that the person feels compelled to avoid. | An obsolete term for a disorder causing personal distress and some impairment in functioning but not causing loss of contact with reality or violation of important social norms. |
| An intense fear of being in a situation where immediate escape is not possible or help is not immediately available in case of incapacitating anxiety. | A severe psychological disorder, typically marked by a loss of contact with reality, delusions and/or hallucinations, and a seriously impaired ability to function. |
| An irrational fear and avoidance of social situations in which people believe they might embarrass or humiliate themselves by appearing clumsy, foolish, or incompetent. | A catch-all category; marked by symptoms of schizophrenia that do not conform to the other types or that conform to more than one type. |
| A marked fear of a specific object or situation; a catch-all category for any phobia other than agoraphobia and social phobia. | A generalized feeling of apprehension, fear, and tension that may be associated with a particular object or situation or may be freefloating, not associated with anything specific. |
| An anxiety disorder in which a person suffers from obsessions and/or compulsions. | An anxiety disorder in which people experience excessive anxiety or worry that they find difficult to control. |
| A persistent, recurring, involuntary thought, image, or impulse that invades consciousness and causes great distress. | An attack of overwhelming anxiety, fear, or terror. |

| | |
|---|---|
| compulsion | dissociative identity disorder |
| somatoform disorders | schizophrenia |
| hypochondriasis | hallucination |
| conversion disorder | delusion |
| dissociative disorders | delusion of grandeur |
| dissociative amnesia | delusion of persecution |
| dissociative fugue | inappropriate affect |

| | |
|---|---|
| A dissociative disorder in which two or more distinct personalities occur in the same person, each taking over at different times; also called multiple personality. | A persistent, irresistible, irrational urge to perform an act or ritual repeatedly. |
| A severe psychological disorder characterized by loss of contact with reality, hallucinations, delusions, inappropriate affect, some disturbance in thinking, social withdrawal, and/or other bizarre behaviour. | Disorders in which physical symptoms are present that are due to psychological rather than physical causes. |
| A sensory perception in the absence of any external sensory stimulation; an imaginary sensation. | A somatoform disorder in which persons are preoccupied with their health and convinced they have some serious disorder despite reassurance from doctors to the contrary. |
| A false belief, not generally shared by others in the culture, that cannot be changed despite strong evidence to the contrary. | A somatoform disorder in which a loss of motor or sensory functioning in some part of the body has no physical cause but solves some psychological problem. |
| A false belief that one is a famous person or one who has some great knowledge, ability, or authority. | Disorders in which, under stress, one loses the integration of consciousness, identity, and memories of important personal events. |
| An individual's false belief that a person or group is trying in some way to harm him or her. | A dissociative disorder in which there is a loss of memory for limited periods in one's life or for one's entire personal identity. |
| A symptom common in schizophrenia in which a person's behaviour (including facial expression, tone of voice, and gestures) does not reflect the emotion that would be expected under the circumstances. | A dissociative disorder in which one has a complete loss of memory for one's entire identity, travels away from home, and may assume a new identity. |

| | |
|---|---|
| catatonic schizophrenia | bipolar disorder |
| disorganized schizophrenia | manic episode |
| paranoid schizophrenia | gender-identity disorders |
| diathesis-stress model | personality disorder |
| mood disorders | antisocial personality disorder |
| major depressive disorder | sexual dysfunction |
| seasonal affective disorder (SAD) | paraphilia |

| | |
|---|---|
| A mood disorder in which manic episodes alternate with periods of depression, usually with relatively normal periods in between. | A type of schizophrenia characterized by extreme stillness or stupor and/or periods of great agitation and excitement; a patient may assume an unusual posture and remain in it for long periods. |
| A period of extreme elation, euphoria, and hyperactivity, often accompanied by delusions of grandeur and by hostility if activity is blocked. | The most serious type of schizophrenia, marked by extreme social withdrawal, hallucinations, delusions, silliness, laughter, grotesque mannerisms, and bizarre behaviour. |
| Disorders characterized by a problem accepting one's identity as male or female. | A type of schizophrenia characterized by delusions of grandeur or persecution. |
| A continuing, inflexible, maladaptive pattern of inner experience and behaviour that causes great distress or impaired functioning and differs significantly from the patterns expected in the person's culture. | The idea that people with a constitutional predisposition (diathesis) toward a disorder, such as schizophrenia, may develop the disorder if they are subjected to sufficient environmental stress. |
| A disorder marked by lack of feeling for others; selfish, aggressive, irresponsible behaviour; and willingness to break the law, lie, cheat, or exploit others for personal gain. | Disorders characterized by extreme and unwarranted disturbances in feeling or mood. |
| A persistent or recurrent problem that causes marked distress and that may involve any of the following: sexual desire, sexual arousal or the pleasure associated with sex, or orgasm. | A mood disorder marked by feelings of great sadness, despair, guilt, worthlessness, and hopelessness and, in extreme cases, suicidal intentions. |
| A sexual disorder in which sexual urges, fantasies, and behaviour generally involve children, other nonconsenting partners, nonhuman objects, or the suffering and humiliation of one or one's partner. | A mood disorder in which depression comes and goes with the seasons. |

# 14

## THERAPIES

c. Gestalt Therapy

- Directive Therapy

3. Relationship Therapies: Therapies Emphasizing Interaction with Others

a. Interpersonal Therapy

b. Family and Couple Therapy

c. Group Therapy

d. Group Help of a Different Sort

- Encounter Groups

- Self-help Groups

Module 14.2 Behaviour Therapies: Unlearning the Old, Learning the New

1. Behaviour Modification Techniques Based on Operant Conditioning

a. Token Economies

b. Time Out

c. Stimulus Satiation

d. The Effectiveness of Operant Approaches

2. Therapies Based on Classical Conditioning

a. Systematic Desensitization

b. Flooding

c. Exposure and Response Prevention

d. Aversion Therapy

3. Therapies Based on Observational Learning

- Participant Modelling

| Module 14.3 Cognitive Therapies: It's the Thought That Counts | 1. Rational-Emotion Therapy: Human Misery—The Legacy of False Beliefs |
| --- | --- |

**The ABCs of Albert Ellis's Rational-Emotive Therapy**

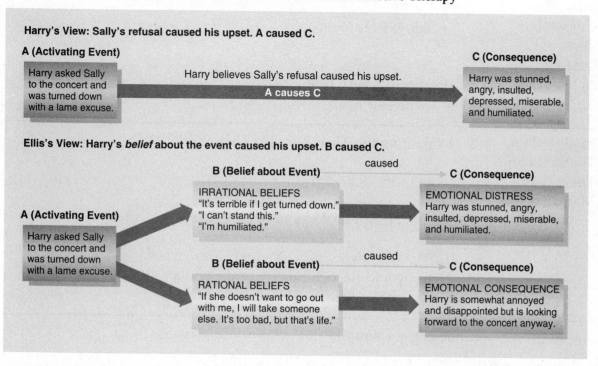

| | |
|---|---|
| | 2. Beck's Cognitive Therapy: Overcoming the "Power of Negative Thinking" |
| | 3. Cognitive Behavioural Therapy: Changes in Thought Change Behaviour |
| Module 14.4 Eye Movement Desensitization and Reprocessing (EMDR) | |
| Module 14.5 The Biological Therapies | 1. Drug Therapy: Pills for Psychological Ills |
| |    a. Antipsychotic Drugs |
| |    b. Antidepressant Drugs |
| |    c. Lithium |
| |    d. The Minor Tranquillizers |
| |    e. Some Problems with Drug Therapy |
| | 2. Electroconvulsive Therapy: The Controversy Continues |
| |    • Side Effects |
| | 3. Psychosurgery: Cutting to Cure |
| Module 14.6 Therapies and Therapists: Many Choices | 1. Evaluating the Therapies: Do They Work? |
| | 2. Mental Health Professionals: How Do They Differ? |
| | 3. Therapy and Race, Ethnicity, and Gender |
| Apply It! | Choosing a Therapist |

**hapter Learning Objective Questions**

Answer the following questions in the space provided and check your answers on the page numbers listed.

| | |
|---|---|
| 14.1 What are the four basic techniques of psychoanalysis, and how are they used to help disturbed patients? p. 440 | |
| 14.2 What is the role of the therapist in person-centred therapy? p. 442 | |
| 14.3 What is the major emphasis in Gestalt therapy? p. 443 | |
| 14.4 What four problems commonly associated with major depression is interpersonal therapy designed to treat? p. 443 | |
| 14.5 What are some advantages of group therapy? p. 444 | |
| 14.6 What is behaviour therapy? p. 446 | |
| 14.7 How do behaviour therapists modify behaviour using operant conditioning techniques? p. 446 | |
| 14.8 What behaviour therapies are based on classical conditioning? p. 447 | |
| 14.9 How do therapists use systematic desensitization to rid people of fears? p. 447 | |
| 14.10 What is flooding? p. 448 | |

14.11 How is exposure and response prevention used to treat people with obsessive-compulsive disorder? p. 448

14.12 How does aversion therapy rid people of a harmful or undesirable behaviour? p. 449

14.13 How does participant modelling help people overcome fears? p. 449

14.14 What is the aim of rational-emotive therapy? p. 451

14.15 How does Beck's cognitive therapy help people overcome depression and anxiety disorders? p. 452

14.16 What is EMDR? p. 454

14.17 What are the three main biological therapies? p. 455

14.18 How do antipsychotic drugs help schizophrenic patients? p. 455

14.19 For what conditions are antidepressants prescribed? p. 456

14.20 How does lithium help patients with bipolar disorder? p. 456

| 14.21 What are some of the problems with drug therapy? p. 457 | |
| --- | --- |

| 14.22 For what purpose is electro-convulsive therapy (ECT) used, and what is its major side effect? p. 457 | |
| --- | --- |

| 14.23 What is psychosurgery, and for what problems is it used? p. 458 | |
| --- | --- |

| 14.24 What different types of mental health professionals conduct psychotherapy? p. 460 | |
| --- | --- |

| 14.25 Why is it important to consider multicultural variables in the therapeutic setting? p. 461 | |
| --- | --- |

After studying the text and completing the Study Guide activities, answer these questions to determine if you need to review any areas before your exam.

1. The treatment of emotional and behavioural disorders with psychological rather than biological methods is known as:
   a. psychotherapy.
   b. psychosurgery.
   c. psychoneuroimmunology.
   d. psychiatry.

2. Psychoanalysts believe that all maladaptive behaviour results from:
   a. an ineffective ego.
   b. unconscious conflicts.
   c. a fixation at an early stage of psycho-sexual development.
   d. overuse of defence mechanisms.

3. Urging a client to express thoughts and feelings freely and to verbalize whatever comes to mind without editing or censoring is a technique called:
   a. transference.
   b. interpretation.
   c. abreaction.
   d. free association.

4. Jamie feels very angry toward her psychoanalyst, which is very similar to the feelings she had toward her father. This expression of hatred toward the analyst is an example of:
   a. free association.
   b. transference.
   c. resistance.
   d. repression.

5. The central task of person-centred therapy involves:
   a. replacing irrational thoughts with rational ones.
   b. creating a warm, accepting climate so that the client's natural tendency toward growth will be realized.
   c. replacing repression with insight.
   d. applying the principles of operant and classical conditioning in psychotherapy.

6. Person-centred therapy is best described as:
   a. confrontive.
   b. structured.
   c. nondirective.
   d. objective.

7. Which therapeutic approach seeks to help a person deal with basic aspects of life, its meaning, and its worth?
   a. Gestalt therapy
   b. interpersonal therapy
   c. group therapy
   d. existential therapy

8. A major goal of Gestalt therapy is to:
   a. get people in touch with their feelings.
   b. help people develop critical thinking skills.
   c. overcome barriers that block the path to self-actualization.
   d. teach people to use anxiety in constructive ways.

9. Interpersonal therapy, also called IPT, is successful to a larger extent because it is:
   a. focused on a specific goal.
   b. free of behaviour modification techniques.
   c. quite long and thorough.
   d. based on a complete re-education of the individual.

10. _____ involves an individual acting out his or her problem relationships with other members of the group playing the significant parts.
    a. Interpersonal therapy
    b. Gestalt therapy
    c. Psychodrama
    d. Token economy

11. Behaviour therapists assume that many distressing psychological problems result from faulty:
    a. defence mechanisms
    b. biochemistry.
    c. reasoning.
    d. learning.

12. Operant conditioning is involved with which of the following?
    a. An event causing an inappropriate positive response is paired with electric shock.
    b. An event causing inappropriate fear is paired with relaxation.
    c. A model demonstrates appropriate action toward a previously feared stimulus.
    d. Positive reinforcers are provided to encourage the performance of desired behaviour.

13. A token economy is involved in which of the following?
    a. Upon performing desired behaviours, a patient receives tokens that can be exchanged for various reinforcers.
    b. An event causing inappropriate fear is paired with relaxation.
    c. An event causing an inappropriate positive response is paired with electric shock.
    d. A situation in which the client provides token appropriate behaviours as a disguise for resistance to therapy.

14. Systematic desensitization is used in the treatment of:
    a. schizophrenia.
    b. mood disorders.
    c. phobias.
    d. somatoform disorders.

15. The technique of flooding is used in which of the following?
    a. direct exposure to feared object without relaxation
    b. imagining painful or sickening stimuli associated with undesirable behaviour
    c. deep muscle relaxation and gradual exposure to feared object
    d. imitating a model responding appropriately in the feared situation

16. Jim wants to quit smoking and tries a technique that involves smoking so much that he feels sick to his stomach. This technique is called:
    a. aversion therapy.
    b. operant therapy.
    c. systematic desensitization.
    d. Gestalt therapy.

17. Albert Ellis believes that abnormal behaviour is caused by:
    a. genetic vulnerability.
    b. irrational behaviour patterns.
    c. irrational thought patterns.
    d. traumatic experiences.

18. What does Aaron Beck call the unreasonable but unquestioned ideas that rule a person's life?
    a. distorted concepts
    b. automatic thoughts
    c. tunnel thinking
    d. thinking tyrants

19. Which of the following is NOT a biological therapy?
    a. ECT
    b. drug therapy
    c. cognitive restructuring
    d. psychosurgery

20. Which of the following drug categories relieves a wide range of symptoms, including hallucinations, delusions, and agitation?
    a. antipsychotics
    b. minor tranquillizers
    c. antidepressants
    d. lithium

21. A patient whose major symptom is a disturbance of mood would probably be prescribed:
    a. antidepressants.
    b. antipsychotics.
    c. major tranquillizers.
    d. antianxiety drugs.

# Answers to Multiple-Choice Questions

| Question Number | Answer | Learning Objective | Explanation for application questions |
|---|---|---|---|
| 1. | a. | 14.1 | |
| 2. | b. | 14.1 | |
| 3. | d. | 14.1 | |
| 4. | b. | 14.1 | |
| 5. | b. | 14.2 | |
| 6. | c. | 14.2 | |
| 7. | d. | 14.2 | |
| 8. | a. | 14.3 | |
| 9. | a. | 14.4 | |
| 10. | c. | 14.4 | |
| 11. | d. | 14.6 | |
| 12. | d. | 14.7 | |
| 13. | a. | 14.7 | |
| 14. | c. | 14.9 | |
| 15. | a. | 14.10 | |
| 16. | a. | 14.12 | |
| 17. | c. | 14.14 | |
| 18. | b. | 14.15 | |
| 19. | c. | 14.17 | |
| 20. | a. | 14.18 | |
| 21. | a. | 14.19 | |

# Glossary for Text Language Enhancement

Students identified the following words from the text as needing more explanation. This page can be cut out, folded in half, and used as a bookmark for this chapter.

| term | definition |
| --- | --- |
| voyeur | pleasure is gained from knowing that those who you watch do not know you are watching them |
| portability | able to move it around easily |
| anonymity | nameless |
| spilling your heart | telling what is very important to you |
| trivial | of little importance |
| balks | resists |
| stark | dramatic |
| facade | pretence; a false front |
| badgers | to torment |
| desensitization | to make less sensitive |
| hierarchy | step-by-step process |
| impotence | man not being able to have sex |
| frigidity | woman not being interested in sex |
| syllabus | course outline |
| rituals | repeating a certain behaviour |
| nausea | uneasy stomach |
| retch | start to vomit |
| abstinence | not drinking any alcohol |
| scenario | situation |
| stunned | shocked, upset |
| dragged on | went slowly |
| confrontational | challenging |
| relapse | get symptoms again |
| catastrophic | horrible |
| delusions | false beliefs |
| hallucinations | sensations that are imaginary |
| fidgeting | moving around too much |
| shuffling gait | walking in small steps |
| mania | excited state |
| advocates | people in favour of |
| deteriorated | became worse |
| apathy | not caring about anything |
| irreversible | cannot go back to the original state |

# Thinking Critically

## Evaluation

In your opinion, what are the major strengths and weaknesses of the following approaches to therapy: insight therapy, behaviour therapy, cognitive therapy, and drug therapy?

## Point/Counterpoint

From what you have learned in this chapter, prepare a strong argument to support each of these positions:

a. Psychotherapy is generally superior to drug therapy in the treatment of psychological disorders.

b. Drug therapy is generally superior to psychotherapy in the treatment of psychological disorders.

## Psychology in Your Life

What questions would you ask a therapist before beginning treatment?

| | |
|---|---|
| psychotherapy | self-actualization |
| insight therapy | non-directive therapy |
| psychoanalysis | Gestalt therapy |
| free association | directive therapy |
| resistance | interpersonal therapy (IPT) |
| transference | family therapy |
| person-centred therapy | group therapy |

| | |
|---|---|
| Developing to one's fullest potential. | Treatment for psychological disorders that uses psychological rather than biological means and primarily involves conversations between patient and therapist. |
| An approach in which the therapist acts to facilitate growth, giving understanding and support rather than proposing solutions, answering questions, or actively directing the course of therapy. | Any type of psychotherapy based on the notion that psychological well-being depends on self-understanding. |
| A therapy originated by Fritz Perls and emphasizing the importance of clients fully experiencing, in the present moment, their feelings, thoughts, and actions and taking personal responsibility for behaviour. | The psychotherapy that uses free association, dream analysis, and analysis of resistance and transference to uncover repressed memories, impulses, and conflicts thought to cause psychological disorders. |
| An approach to therapy in which the therapist takes an active role in determining the course of therapy sessions and provides answers and suggestions to the patients. | A psychoanalytic technique used to explore the unconscious by having patients reveal whatever thoughts or images come to mind. |
| A brief psychotherapy designed to help depressed people understand their problems in interpersonal relationships and develop ways to improve them. | In psychoanalytic therapy, the patient's attempts to avoid expressing or revealing painful or embarrassing thoughts or feelings. |
| Therapy based on the assumption that an individual's problem is caused and/or maintained in part by problems within the family unit, and so the entire family is involved in therapy. | An intense emotional situation occurring in psychoanalysis, when one comes to behave toward the analyst as one had behaved toward a significant figure from the past. |
| A form of therapy in which several clients (usually 7–10) meet regularly with one or two therapists to resolve personal problems. | A nondirective, humanistic therapy in which the therapist creates a warm, accepting climate, freeing clients to be themselves and releasing their natural tendency toward positive growth. |

| | |
|---|---|
| psychodrama | systematic desensitization |
| encounter group | flooding |
| behaviour therapy | exposure and response prevention |
| behaviour modification | aversion therapy |
| token economy | participant modelling |
| time out | cognitive therapy |
| stimulus satiation | rational-emotive therapy |

| | |
|---|---|
| A behaviour therapy, used to treat phobias, that teaches deep muscle relaxation with gradual exposure to the anxiety-producing situations until the patient can remain relaxed. | A group therapy in which one group member acts out personal problems, situations, and relationships, assisted by other members, to gain insight into the problem. |
| A behavioural therapy used to treat phobias, during which clients are exposed to the feared object or event (or asked to imagine it vividly) for an extended period until their anxiety decreases. | An intense emotional group experience designed to promote personal growth and self-knowledge; participants are encouraged to let down their defences and relate honestly and openly to one another. |
| A behaviour therapy that exposes obsessive-compulsive disorder patients to stimuli generating anxiety; patients must agree not to carry out their normal rituals for a specified period of time after exposure. | A treatment approach using operant conditioning, classical conditioning, and/or observation learning theory to eliminate inappropriate or maladaptive behaviours and replace them with more adaptive responses. |
| A behaviour therapy in which an aversive stimulus is paired with an undesirable behaviour until the behaviour becomes associated with pain and discomfort. | The systematic application of learning principles to help a person eliminate undesirable behaviours and/or acquire more adaptive behaviours; sometimes this term is used interchangeably with behaviour therapy. |
| A behaviour therapy in which an appropriate response is modelled in graduated steps and the client attempts each step, encouraged and supported by the therapist. | A behavioural technique used to encourage desirable behaviours by reinforcing them with tokens that can be exchanged later for desired objects, activities, and/or privileges. |
| Any therapy designed to change maladaptive thoughts and behaviour based on the assumption that maladaptive behaviour can result from irrational thoughts, beliefs, and ideas. | A behavioural technique, used to decrease the frequency of undesirable behaviour, that involves withdrawing an individual from all reinforcement for a period of time. |
| A directive, confrontational therapy designed to challenge and modify the irrational beliefs thought to cause personal distress; developed by Albert Ellis. | A behavioural technique in which a patient is given so much of a stimulus he or she finds reinforcing that it becomes something the patient wants to avoid. |

| | |
|---|---|
| relationship theories | |
| automatic thoughts | lobotomy |
| Beck's cognitive therapy | clinical psychologist |
| antipsychotic drugs | psychiatrist |
| antidepressants | psychoanalyst |
| cognitive behavioural therapy (CBT) | biological therapy |
| electroconvulsive therapy | unconditionaol positive regard |
| psychosurgery | existential therapy |

| | Therapies that look not only at individual struggles but also at inter-personal relationships. |
|---|---|
| A psychosurgery technique in which the nerve fibres connecting the frontal lobes to the deeper brain centres are severed. | Unreasonable and unquestioned ideas that rule a person's life and lead to depression and anxiety. |
| A psychologist, usually with a Ph.D., whose training is in the diagnosis, treatment, or research of psychological and behavioural disorders. | A brief therapy for depression and anxiety, which helps people recognize their automatic thoughts and replace them with more objective thoughts. |
| A medical doctor with a speciality in the diagnosis and treatment of mental disorders. | Drugs used to control severe psychotic symptoms, such as the delusions and hallucinations of schizophrenics; also known as neuroleptics or major tranquillizers. |
| A professional, usually a psychiatrist, with special training in psycho-analysis. | Drugs that are prescribed to treat depression and some anxiety disorders. |
| A therapy, based on the assumption that most mental disorders have physical causes, that attempts to change the biological mechanism involved. | A therapy based on the belief that changing how a person thinks about a situation can result in changes in how a person feels and behaves in that situation. |
| A condition required of person-centred therapists, involving a caring for and acceptance of clients regardless of the clients' feelings, thoughts, or behaviours. | A treatment in which an electric current is passed through the brain, causing a seizure; usually reserved for the severely depressed who are either suicidal or unresponsive to other treatment. |
| A therapy that places an emphasis on finding meaning in life. | Brain surgery to treat some severe, persistent, and debilitating psychological disorder or severe chronic pain. |

# Notes:

# Notes: